APPETIZERS
FOR EVERY SEASON

TASTE OF HOME BOOKS • RDA ENTHUSIAST BRANDS, LLC • MILWAUKEE, WI

© 2021 RDA Enthusiast Brands, LLC.
1610 N. 2nd St., Suite 102,
Milwaukee WI 53212-3906

Visit us at **tasteofhome.com** for other
Taste of Home books and products.

International Standard Book Number:
978-1-61765-983-6
Library of Congress Control Number:
2020936339
Component Number: 118600100H

Executive Editor: Mark Hagen
Senior Art Director: Raeann Thompson
Designers: Arielle Jardine, Jazmin Delgado
Copy Editor: Sara Strauss

Cover Photography:
Taste of Home Photo Studio
Pictured on front cover:
Cheesy Meatball Sliders, p. 81
Pictured on title page:
Cilantro Tomato Bruschetta, p. 85
Pictured on back cover:
Slow-Cooker Cheese Dip, p. 82
So Very Berry Brie, p. 86
Zucchini & Cheese Roulades, p. 90
Pictured on spine:
Risotto Balls (Arancini), p. 218

Printed in Malaysia
1 3 5 7 9 10 8 6 4 2

42

148

135

186

36

CONTENTS

MORE WAYS TO CONNECT WITH US:

KEEP THE PARTY GOING ALL YEAR

Make your home the neighborhood hot spot when you stock buffets with the finger foods everyone craves. Whether hosting a backyard barbecue or a holiday open house, you'll always find the ideal bite in this handy cookbook!

58

There's always a need for crowd-pleasing appetizers, snacks and hors d'oeuvres—no matter what the party, occasion or time of year. Now you can serve up the savory nibbles that keep everyone happily munching through any party. Welcome spring with fresh, colorful veggies and thick creamy dips; toast summer with trays of fiery favorites; serve bowls of crunchy mixes in fall; and deck the halls with Christmas standbys everyone adores.

Take a look inside, and you'll discover that each season features a selection of both cold and hot appetizers, making it easier than ever to find the perfect nibble. Consider a no-bake bite for informal gatherings or last-minute fun, and whip up an oven-fresh nibble when something more formal is needed. From quick, casual noshes to truly impressive specialties, ***Taste of Home Appetizers for Every Season*** always has the answer.

112

177

107

THE PERFECT PARTY IS EASILY WITHIN REACH

Hosting a family holiday? Having a few friends over for game night? A great get-together all comes down to a bit of planning on your part.

This cookbook makes it a snap to throw a party. Start organizing your event by selecting a combination of hot and cold appetizers. Turn to the applicable season in this book, and you'll find an index that can help you create an outstanding lineup.

Next, use this book's icons to find the bites that work with your schedule.

🕐 These fast-fix snacks come together in just 30 minutes or less.

5️⃣ You need only five items for these party starters—not including water, salt, pepper, oils or optional ingredients.

❄️ Stash a few of these make-ahead bites in the freezer for quick party prep.

Check the time requirements of each dish so you're not overwhelmed on the day of your gathering.

Try to consider the number of appetizers you'll need. This number will vary by the type of event you're hosting.

SERVING SUGGESTIONS

- For cocktails before dinner, plan 3 to 4 different party starters and 4 to 5 pieces per person.
- For an open-house buffet, serve 4 to 5 hors d'oeuvres and 4 to 6 pieces per guest.
- For a light dinner of finger foods, plan 6 to 8 types of appetizers and roughly 14 to 16 pieces per person.

It's often best to serve warm finger foods by baking and serving them in batches. Cold items can be made ahead, tightly wrapped and kept in the refrigerator to replenish as needed.

Take cheese balls and dips that contain cream cheese out of the fridge about 15 minutes before serving for the best texture and flavor.

Do's and Don'ts for Today's Hostesses

Run through this quick list before your guests arrive.

- Do play music in the background to set the mood, but quiet enough to allow for conversation.
- Do create an open floor plan so guests can easily walk from one room to the next.
- Do set up chairs in arrangements that encourage conversation.
- Don't stash the trash containers but set them out strategically to prevent clutter from building up.
- Don't hide the coasters if you want your guests to use them. Have plenty available, and place them in noticeable locations.
- Don't keep clutter on tables and on other surfaces. Give guests room to easily set down their glasses and plates.

GREEK VEGGIE
TARTLETS, 67

SPRING

It's in the air and on your table thanks to the breezy selection of hot and cold bites in this chapter. How refreshing!

HOT

COLD

SANTORINI LAMB SLIDERS

I love lamb burgers, so I created a crowd-friendly slider version.
The tzatziki sauce is best made a day or two in advance to allow the flavors to mingle.
—*Cristina Certano, Colorado Springs, CO*

PREP: 30 min. + chilling • **GRILL:** 10 min. • **MAKES:** 10 servings

1   cup plain Greek yogurt
½   cup shredded peeled cucumber
1¼ tsp. salt, divided
1   lb. ground lamb
1   Tbsp. grated lemon zest
4   garlic cloves, minced and divided
2   tsp. dried oregano
¼   tsp. plus ⅛ tsp. pepper, divided
1   tsp. lemon juice
1   tsp. dill weed
10 mini buns or mini ciabatta buns
10 Bibb lettuce leaves or Boston lettuce leaves
1   medium red onion, thinly sliced
1   cup crumbled feta cheese

1. Line a strainer or colander with 4 layers of cheesecloth or 1 coffee filter; place over a bowl. Place Greek yogurt in the prepared strainer; cover yogurt with the sides of cheesecloth. Refrigerate 2-4 hours. Meanwhile, place cucumber in a colander over a plate; sprinkle with ¼ tsp. salt and toss. Let stand 30 minutes.

2. For burgers, in a large bowl, combine lamb, lemon zest, 2 garlic cloves, oregano, ¾ tsp. salt and ¼ tsp. pepper, mixing lightly but thoroughly. Shape into ten ½-in.-thick patties. Refrigerate 30 minutes.

3. For sauce, remove yogurt from cheesecloth to a bowl; discard strained liquid. Squeeze cucumber; blot dry with paper towels. Add cucumber, lemon juice, dill, remaining 2 garlic cloves, remaining ¼ tsp. salt and remaining ⅛ tsp. pepper to yogurt, stirring until combined.

4. Grill the burgers, covered, over medium heat for 3-4 minutes on each side or until a thermometer reads 160°. Grill mini buns over medium heat, cut sides down, for 30-60 seconds or until toasted. Serve burgers on buns with lettuce, red onion, feta and sauce.

1 SLIDER: 228 cal., 12g fat (5g sat. fat), 43mg chol., 531mg sod., 16g carb. (3g sugars, 1g fiber), 14g pro.

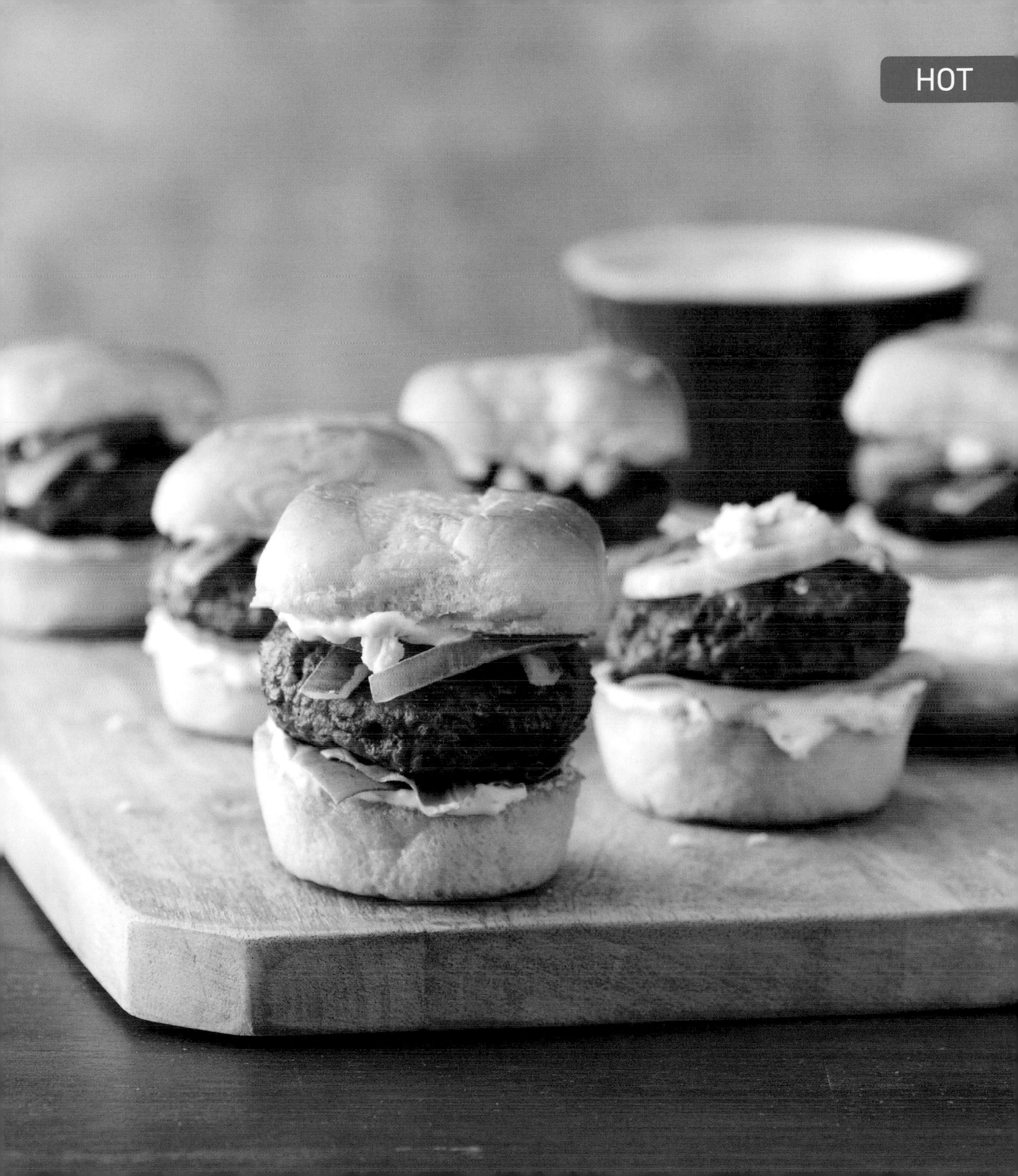

⏱ ❄ ARTICHOKE PHYLLO CUPS

One of my favorite appetizers (which I find addicting!) is spinach and artichoke dip. My bite-sized version captures all of that savory richness in a baked phyllo cup.
—*Neel Patel, Champaign, IL*

TAKES: 30 min. • **MAKES:** about 3½ dozen

3 pkg. (1.9 oz. each) frozen miniature phyllo tart shells
1 can (14 oz.) water-packed artichoke hearts, rinsed, drained and finely chopped
½ cup shredded part-skim mozzarella cheese
3 green onions, chopped
¼ cup whipped cream cheese
2 Tbsp. minced fresh parsley
2 Tbsp. grated Parmesan cheese
2 Tbsp. sour cream
1 Tbsp. mayonnaise
2 garlic cloves, minced
½ tsp. salt
¼ tsp. pepper

1. Place tart shells on a baking sheet. In a small bowl, combine the remaining ingredients; spoon into shells.

2. Bake at 350° until lightly browned, 10-15 minutes. Serve warm.

FREEZE OPTION: Freeze cooled baked pastries in freezer containers, separating layers with waxed paper. To use, reheat pastries on a baking sheet in a preheated 350° oven until heated through.

1 APPETIZER: 70 cal., 4g fat (1g sat. fat), 4mg chol., 149mg sod., 6g carb. (0 sugars, 0 fiber), 2g pro.

READER RAVE

"I couldn't believe how easy these were to prepare, and they were gobbled up instantly at the party I took them to. I left a few at the house for my children. When I returned, the kids begged me to make another batch."
—7833LOUISE, TASTEOFHOME.COM

HOT WINGS

For most people, these wings seem to have just the right amount of zip. If you want them a little hotter—as we often do—simply add more hot pepper sauce.
—*Dawn Wright, Moline, MI*

PREP: 45 min. + standing • **BAKE:** 15 min. • **MAKES:** 40 servings

4 **lbs. whole chicken wings**
Oil for deep-fat frying
¼ **cup butter**
¼ **cup honey**
¼ **cup barbecue sauce**
4 **to 6 Tbsp. hot pepper sauce**
3 **Tbsp. vinegar**
3 **Tbsp. prepared mustard**
¼ **tsp. garlic salt**
Celery and carrot sticks
Blue cheese or ranch salad dressing

1. Cut wings into 3 sections; discard wing tip section. In a deep cast-iron or electric skillet, heat oil to 350°. Fry wings, a few at a time, about 9 minutes or until golden. Drain on paper towels; place in a large bowl.

2. In a small saucepan, combine the next 7 ingredients; cook and stir 5-10 minutes. Pour over cooked wings; let stand 10 minutes. With a slotted spoon, remove wings from the sauce and place them in a single layer on greased baking sheets.

3. Bake at 350° for 15 minutes. Serve hot with vegetable sticks and dressing for dipping.

1 PIECE: 92 cal., 7g fat (2g sat. fat), 15mg chol., 72mg sod., 3g carb. (2g sugars, 0 fiber), 4g pro.

❄ RAVIOLI APPETIZER POPS

Ravioli on a stick is a tasty appetizer everyone talks about. It's simple and fun!
Use ready-made dipping sauces, or create your own.
—*Erika Monroe-Williams, Scottsdale, AZ*

PREP: 25 min. • **COOK:** 5 min./batch • **MAKES:** 3½ dozen

½   **cup dry bread crumbs**
2   **tsp. pepper**
1½ **tsp. dried oregano**
1½ **tsp. dried parsley flakes**
1   **tsp. salt**
1   **tsp. crushed red pepper flakes**
⅓   **cup all-purpose flour**
2   **large eggs, lightly beaten**
1   **pkg. (9 oz.) refrigerated cheese ravioli**
    Oil for frying
    Grated Parmesan cheese, optional
42 **lollipop sticks**
    Warm marinara sauce and prepared pesto

1. In a shallow bowl, mix the dry bread crumbs and seasonings. Place flour and eggs in separate shallow bowls. Dip ravioli in flour to coat both sides; shake off excess. Dip in egg, then in crumb mixture, patting to help coating adhere.

2. In a large electric or cast-iron skillet, heat ½ in. of oil to 375°. Fry the ravioli, a few at a time, until golden brown, 1-2 minutes on each side. Drain on paper towels. Immediately sprinkle with cheese if desired. Carefully insert a lollipop stick into the back of each ravioli. Serve warm with marinara sauce and pesto.

1 APPETIZER: 32 cal., 1g fat (0 sat. fat), 9mg chol., 97mg sod., 4g carb. (0 sugars, 0 fiber), 1g pro.

TEST KITCHEN TIP

Make these ahead and stash them in the freezer for fast bites. Fry a batch as directed and freeze in a single layer. To reheat, pop a few in a 425° oven and bake until crispy.

TUSCAN SAUSAGE & BEAN DIP

This is a spinoff of a Mexican dip I once had. The original was really good, but I was going through an I'm-so-over-Mexican-dip phase and decided to switch things up. Take this version to a party—I'll bet no one else brings anything like it!

—Mandy Rivers, Lexington, SC

PREP: 25 min. • **BAKE:** 20 min. • **MAKES:** 16 servings

1 **lb. bulk hot Italian sausage**
1 **medium onion, finely chopped**
4 **garlic cloves, minced**
½ **cup dry white wine or chicken broth**
½ **tsp. dried oregano**
¼ **tsp. salt**
¼ **tsp. dried thyme**
1 **pkg. (8 oz.) cream cheese, softened**
1 **pkg. (6 oz.) fresh baby spinach, coarsely chopped**
1 **can (15 oz.) cannellini beans, rinsed and drained**
1 **cup chopped seeded tomatoes**
1 **cup shredded part-skim mozzarella cheese**
½ **cup shredded Parmesan cheese**
Assorted crackers or toasted French bread baguette slices

1. Preheat oven to 375°. In a large skillet, cook Italian sausage, onion and garlic over medium heat until sausage is no longer pink, breaking up sausage into crumbles; drain. Stir in wine, oregano, salt and thyme. Bring to a boil; cook until liquid is almost evaporated.

2. Add cream cheese; stir until melted. Stir in spinach, beans and tomatoes; cook and stir until spinach is wilted. Transfer to a greased 8-in. square baking dish; if using an ovenproof skillet, leave in skillet. Sprinkle with cheeses.

3. Bake until bubbly, 20-25 minutes. Serve with crackers.

¼ CUP: 200 cal., 14g fat (7g sat. fat), 41mg chol., 434mg sod., 7g carb. (2g sugars, 2g fiber), 10g pro.

CILANTRO & LIME CHICKEN WITH SCOOPS

I created this recipe when I was preparing for a large party and wanted a healthy Tex-Mex chicken option. While it's in the slow cooker, I can turn my attention to other dishes. Enjoy leftovers in a green salad or wrapped in tortillas for burritos.
—*Lori Terry, Chicago, IL*

PREP: 15 min. • **COOK:** 3½ hours • **MAKES:** 16 servings (4 cups)

1 **lb. boneless skinless chicken breasts**

2 **tsp. chili powder**

2 **Tbsp. lime juice**

1½ **cups frozen petite corn (about 5 oz.), thawed**

1½ **cups chunky salsa**

1½ **cups (6 oz.) finely shredded cheddar cheese**

1 **medium sweet red pepper, finely chopped**

4 **green onions, thinly sliced**

Minced fresh cilantro

Baked tortilla chip scoops

1. Place chicken in a 1½-qt. slow cooker; sprinkle with chili powder and lime juice. Cook, covered, on low until tender, 3-4 hours.

2. Remove chicken; discard cooking juices. Shred chicken with 2 forks; return to the slow cooker. Add corn and salsa; cook, covered, on low until heated through, about 30 minutes, stirring occasionally.

3. Transfer to a large bowl; stir in cheese, pepper and green onions. Sprinkle with cilantro; serve with tortilla chip scoops.

¼ CUP CHICKEN MIXTURE: 97 cal., 4g fat (2g sat. fat), 26mg chol., 183mg sod., 5g carb. (2g sugars, 1g fiber), 9g pro.

DIABETIC EXCHANGES: 1 medium-fat meat.

BEEF & ONION PIROSHKI

One of my favorite places in Seattle is a small stand that sells piroshki—Russian stuffed pocket sandwiches. Whenever I have a craving, I simply make my own batch.
—*Julie Merriman, Seattle, WA*

PREP: 30 min. + cooling • **BAKE:** 15 min. • **MAKES:** 32 appetizers

1 lb. lean ground beef (90% lean)
1 cup finely chopped sweet onion
2 garlic cloves, minced
½ tsp. salt
¼ tsp. pepper
1 cup chopped fresh spinach
1 cup shredded Havarti cheese
¼ cup sour cream
2 Tbsp. snipped fresh dill
1 pkg. (17.3 oz.) frozen puff pastry, thawed
1 large egg
1 Tbsp. water

1. In a large skillet, cook beef, onion, garlic, salt and pepper over medium heat until meat is no longer pink; drain. Cool to room temperature.

2. Stir spinach, cheese, sour cream and dill into beef mixture. On a lightly floured surface, roll a puff pastry sheet into a 12-in. square. Cut into sixteen 3-in. squares. Repeat with remaining sheet.

3. Spoon 1 Tbsp. beef mixture onto the center of each square. Fold dough over filling, forming a triangle; press edges with a fork to seal. Transfer to greased baking sheets. Whisk egg and water; brush over tops. Bake at 400° until golden brown, 14-16 minutes.

1 APPETIZER: 115 cal., 6g fat (2g sat. fat), 18mg chol., 118mg sod., 9g carb. (0 sugars, 1g fiber), 5g pro.

HOT

🕐 HEARTY RYE MELTS

When we moved from the Midwest to Kentucky, we were invited to a neighborhood gathering, where we discovered this appetizer. Hanky panky, as it's often called here, is traditionally served at Derby Day parties. In our house, it's become a year-round favorite.
—*Melanie Schlaf, Edgewood, KY*

TAKES: 30 min. • **MAKES:** 2 dozen

½ lb. lean ground beef (90% lean)
½ lb. bulk pork sausage
1½ tsp. chili powder
8 oz. Velveeta, shredded
24 slices snack rye bread
Fresh parsley sprigs, stems removed

1. In a large skillet, cook beef and sausage over medium heat until no longer pink; drain. Add chili powder and cheese; cook and stir until cheese is melted. Spread a heaping tablespoonful on each slice of bread. Place on a baking sheet.

2. Bake at 350° for 12-15 minutes or until edges of bread begin to crisp. Garnish with parsley. Serve warm.

1 PIECE: 88 cal., 6g fat (2g sat. fat), 20mg chol., 231mg sod., 4g carb. (1g sugars, 0 fiber), 5g pro.

HOT SPINACH SPREAD WITH PITA CHIPS

Bubbly and cheesy, this spread is absolutely scrumptious on toasted pita wedges.
Its colorful appearance makes a stunning addition to any buffet.
—*Teresa Emanuel, Smithville, MO*

. . . .

PREP: 30 min. • **BAKE:** 20 min. • **MAKES:** 16 servings (4 cups spread)

2 cups shredded Monterey Jack cheese

1 pkg. (10 oz.) frozen chopped spinach, thawed and squeezed dry

1 pkg. (8 oz.) cream cheese, cubed

2 plum tomatoes, seeded and chopped

¾ cup chopped onion

⅓ cup half-and-half cream

1 Tbsp. finely chopped seeded jalapeno pepper

6 pita breads (6 in.)

½ cup butter, melted

2 tsp. lemon-pepper seasoning

2 tsp. ground cumin

¼ tsp. garlic salt

1. In a large bowl, combine the first 7 ingredients. Transfer to a greased 1½-qt. baking dish. Bake, uncovered, at 375° for 20-25 minutes or until bubbly.

2. Meanwhile, cut each pita bread into 8 wedges. Place in two 15x10x1-in. baking pans. Combine butter, lemon pepper, cumin and garlic salt; brush over pita wedges.

3. Bake for 7-9 minutes or until crisp. Serve with the spinach spread.

¼ CUP SPREAD WITH 3 PITA WEDGES: 231 cal., 16g fat (10g sat. fat), 46mg chol., 381mg sod., 15g carb. (1g sugars, 1g fiber), 8g pro.

HOT

ALMOND-BACON CHEESE CROSTINI

Try these baked bites when you want a change from the usual toasted tomato appetizer. For an elegant presentation, slice the baguette at an angle instead of making a straight cut.
—*Leondre Hermann, Stuart, FL*

PREP: 30 min. • **BAKE:** 15 min. • **MAKES:** 3 dozen

1 French bread baguette (1 lb.), cut into 36 slices
2 cups shredded Monterey Jack cheese
⅔ cup mayonnaise
½ cup sliced almonds, toasted
6 bacon strips, cooked and crumbled
1 green onion, chopped
   Dash salt
   Additional toasted almonds, optional

1. Place bread slices on an ungreased baking sheet. Bake at 400° until lightly browned, 8-9 minutes.

2. Meanwhile, in a large bowl, combine the cheese, mayonnaise, almonds, bacon, onion and salt. Spread over bread. Bake until cheese is melted, 7-8 minutes. Sprinkle with additional almonds if desired. Serve warm.

1 SLICE: 120 cal., 8g fat (2g sat. fat), 8mg chol., 160mg sod., 10g carb. (0 sugars, 1g fiber), 3g pro.

READER RAVE

"Such a tasty and easy appetizer to make. I have changed the cheese flavor or mixed cheeses, and the crostini is still gobbled up every time!"
—RENA55, TASTEOFHOME.COM

CHEESY SKILLET PIZZA DIP

This standout skillet oozes with cheesy goodness thanks to cream cheese and mozzarella. We topped our dip with pepperoni, but you can easily customize it with your favorite pizza toppings. The bonus? This is another way to use your cast-iron pan.
—Taste of Home *Test Kitchen*

PREP: 25 min. + rising • **BAKE:** 25 min. • **MAKES:** 18 servings

6	Tbsp. butter
1	tsp. garlic powder, divided
¼	tsp. crushed red pepper flakes
1	pkg. (16 oz.) frozen bread dough dinner rolls, thawed
1	pkg. (8 oz.) cream cheese, softened
1½	cups shredded part-skim mozzarella cheese, divided
1	cup mayonnaise
1	tsp. Italian seasoning
½	cup pizza sauce
¼	cup (¾ oz.) sliced pepperoni
2	Tbsp. shredded Parmesan cheese
2	Tbsp. minced fresh basil

1. Microwave butter, ½ tsp. garlic powder and red pepper flakes, covered, until butter is melted. Cut each dinner roll into thirds; roll each piece into a ball. Dip dough balls in butter mixture; place along outer edge of a 10-in. cast-iron skillet, leaving center open. Gently stack the remaining balls on top of the bottom layer, leaving some space between them. Cover and let rise until almost doubled, about 30 minutes.

2. Preheat oven to 400°. Bake until dough balls are set and beginning to brown, 15-18 minutes.

3. Meanwhile, combine cream cheese, 1 cup mozzarella, mayonnaise, Italian seasoning and remaining garlic powder; spoon into the center of skillet. Layer with ¼ cup mozzarella and pizza sauce. Top with remaining mozzarella and pepperoni. Brush the rolls with some of remaining butter mixture; sprinkle with Parmesan.

4. Bake until dip is heated through and rolls are golden brown, about 10 minutes, covering loosely with foil as needed to prevent rolls from becoming too dark. Sprinkle with basil.

1 SERVING: 258 cal., 20g fat (7g sat. fat), 29mg chol., 372mg sod., 15g carb. (2g sugars, 1g fiber), 6g pro.

HOT

LOADED PULLED PORK CUPS

Potato nests are simple to create and are perfect for filling with pulled pork, cheese, sour cream and more. Make, bake and collect the compliments!
—*Melissa Sperka, Greensboro, NC*

PREP: 40 min. • **BAKE:** 25 min. • **MAKES:** 1½ dozen

1   pkg. (20 oz.) refrigerated shredded hash brown potatoes
¾   cup shredded Parmesan cheese
2   large egg whites, beaten
1   tsp. garlic salt
½   tsp. onion powder
¼   tsp. pepper
1   carton (16 oz.) refrigerated fully cooked barbecued shredded pork
1   cup shredded Colby-Monterey Jack cheese
½   cup sour cream
5   bacon strips, cooked and crumbled
     Minced chives

1. Preheat oven to 450°. In a large bowl, mix hash browns, Parmesan cheese, egg whites and seasonings until blended. Divide the potato mixture among 18 well-greased muffin cups; press on the bottoms and up the sides to form cups.

2. Bake until the edges of cups are dark golden brown, 22-25 minutes. Carefully run a knife around the sides of each cup. Cool 5 minutes before removing from the pans to a serving platter. Meanwhile, heat pulled pork according to package directions.

3. Sprinkle cheese into cups. Top with pork, sour cream and bacon; sprinkle with chives. Serve warm.

1 PULLED PORK CUP: 129 cal., 6g fat (3g sat. fat), 19mg chol., 439mg sod., 11g carb. (4g sugars, 0 fiber), 8g pro.

TERIYAKI SALMON BUNDLES

Bored with the usual appetizers? Give these a try. For easy dipping, I serve the little bundles on skewers. Standing them in a small vase filled with table salt is a fun presentation.

—*Diane Halferty, Corpus Christi, TX*

PREP: 30 min. • **BAKE:** 20 min. • **MAKES:** 32 appetizers (¾ cup sauce)

4 Tbsp. reduced-sodium teriyaki sauce, divided
½ tsp. grated lemon zest
2 Tbsp. lemon juice
1¼ lbs. salmon fillet, cut into 1-in. cubes
1 pkg. (17.3 oz.) frozen puff pastry, thawed
⅔ cup orange marmalade

1. Preheat oven to 400°. In a large bowl, whisk 2 Tbsp. teriyaki sauce, lemon zest and lemon juice. Add salmon; toss to coat. Marinate at room temperature 20 minutes.

2. Drain salmon, discarding marinade. Unfold puff pastry. Cut each sheet lengthwise into ½-in.-wide strips; cut strips crosswise in half. Overlap 2 strips of pastry, forming an X. Place a salmon cube in the center. Wrap pastry over salmon; pinch ends to seal. Place on a greased baking sheet, seam side down. Repeat. Bake until golden brown, 18-20 minutes.

3. In a small bowl, mix orange marmalade and remaining teriyaki. Serve with salmon bundles.

1 APPETIZER WITH ABOUT 1 TSP. SAUCE: 120 cal., 6g fat (1g sat. fat), 9mg chol., 93mg sod., 13g carb. (4g sugars, 1g fiber), 4g pro.

⏱ 5️⃣ BOURBON MEATBALLS

Kick-start packaged frozen meatballs with a splash of bourbon, vinegar, spicy brown mustard and brown sugar for punchy sweet-and-sour flavor.
—*Kimla Carsten, Grand Junction, CO*

. . . .

TAKES: 30 min. • **MAKES:** about 3½ dozen

2 pkg. (22 oz. each) frozen fully cooked Angus beef meatballs
¾ cup packed brown sugar
¼ cup white vinegar
¼ cup bourbon
2 tsp. spicy brown mustard

1. Prepare meatballs according to package directions.

2. In a large skillet, whisk together remaining ingredients. Bring mixture to a simmer; cook 5 minutes. Stir in the meatballs; simmer until heated through, about 5 minutes.

1 MEATBALL: 95 cal., 6g fat (3g sat. fat), 16mg chol., 192mg sod., 5g carb. (4g sugars, 0 fiber), 4g pro.

TEST KITCHEN TIP

Dark brown sugar contains more molasses than light or golden brown sugar. The types are generally interchangeable in recipes, but if you prefer a bolder flavor, choose dark brown sugar.

REUBEN WAFFLE POTATO APPETIZERS

I love Reubens, so I turned that classic sammie into small bites for an appetizer table. Waffle fries are great for piling on the corned beef, sauerkraut and more.
—*Gloria Bradley, Naperville, IL*

PREP: 30 min. • **BAKE:** 10 min./batch • **MAKES:** about 4 dozen

1 pkg. (22 oz.) frozen waffle-cut fries

4 oz. cream cheese, softened

2 cups shredded fontina cheese, divided

⅓ cup Thousand Island salad dressing

3 Tbsp. chopped sweet onion

1½ tsp. prepared horseradish

12 oz. sliced deli corned beef, coarsely chopped

1 cup sauerkraut, rinsed, well drained and chopped

2 Tbsp. minced fresh chives

1. Prepare waffle fries according to package directions for baking. Meanwhile, in a small bowl, beat cream cheese, 1 cup fontina cheese, salad dressing, onion and horseradish until blended.

2. Remove fries from oven; reduce oven setting to 400°. Top each waffle fry with about ¼ oz. corned beef and 1 tsp. each cream cheese mixture, sauerkraut and remaining fontina cheese. Bake until cheese is melted, 8-10 minutes. Sprinkle with chives.

1 APPETIZER: 62 cal., 4g fat (2g sat. fat), 12mg chol., 168mg sod., 4g carb. (0 sugars, 0 fiber), 3g pro.

🕐 ASPARAGUS BRUSCHETTA

I really like asparagus, so I'm always experimenting with it in different recipes. This is a delicious twist on traditional bruschetta.
—*Elaine Sweet, Dallas, TX*

TAKES: 30 min. • **MAKES:** 1 dozen

3 cups water
½ lb. fresh asparagus, trimmed and cut into ½-in. pieces
2 cups grape tomatoes, halved
¼ cup minced fresh basil
3 green onions, chopped
3 Tbsp. lime juice
1 Tbsp. olive oil
3 garlic cloves, minced
1½ tsp. grated lime zest
¼ tsp. salt
¼ tsp. pepper
12 slices French bread baguette (½ in. thick), toasted
½ cup crumbled blue cheese

1. In a large saucepan, bring water to a boil. Add the asparagus; cover and boil for 2-4 minutes. Drain and immediately place asparagus in ice water. Drain and pat dry.

2. In a large bowl, combine asparagus, tomatoes, basil, onions, lime juice, oil, garlic, lime zest, salt and pepper. Using a slotted spoon, spoon asparagus mixture onto toasted bread. Sprinkle with blue cheese.

1 PIECE: 88 cal., 3g fat (1g sat. fat), 4mg chol., 237mg sod., 13g carb. (1g sugars, 1g fiber), 3g pro.

DIABETIC EXCHANGES: 1 starch, ½ fat.

🕐 CHUNKY BLUE CHEESE DIP

Every time I make this quick dip for a party, someone asks for the recipe.
It requires only a few ingredients and takes just 15 minutes to prepare.
My blue cheese of choice is often Gorgonzola.
—*Sandy Schneider, Naperville, IL*

. . . .

TAKES: 15 min. • **MAKES:** 12 servings

1   pkg. (8 oz.) cream cheese, softened
⅓   cup sour cream
½   tsp. white pepper
¼   to ½ tsp. salt
1   cup crumbled blue cheese
⅓   cup minced fresh chives
     Toasted chopped pecans, optional
     Apple and pear slices

Beat first 4 ingredients until blended; gently stir in blue cheese and chives. Transfer to a serving bowl. If desired, sprinkle with pecans. Serve with apple and pear slices.

2 TBSP. DIP: 112 cal., 10g fat (6g sat. fat), 32mg chol., 229mg sod., 1g carb. (1g sugars, 0 fiber), 3g pro.

TEST KITCHEN TIP

Get creative with this easy dip. Stir in some chopped cooked bacon or slivered almonds. Serve with celery sticks or pitas.

⏱ BEST DEVILED EGGS

Herbs lend amazing flavor to these deviled eggs, which truly are the best you can make!
The recipe includes tasty variations that feature bacon, chipotle peppers and crab.
—*Jesse and Anne Foust, Bluefield, WV*

TAKES: 15 min. • **MAKES:** 2 dozen

½ cup mayonnaise
2 Tbsp. 2% milk
1 tsp. dried parsley flakes
½ tsp. dill weed
½ tsp. minced chives
½ tsp. ground mustard
¼ tsp. salt
¼ tsp. paprika
⅛ tsp. garlic powder
⅛ tsp. pepper
12 hard-boiled large eggs
Minced fresh parsley and additional paprika

In a small bowl, combine the first 10 ingredients. Cut eggs lengthwise in half; remove yolks and set whites aside. In another bowl, mash yolks; add to mayonnaise mixture, mixing well. Spoon or pipe the filling into egg whites. Sprinkle with parsley and additional paprika. Refrigerate until serving.

1 STUFFED EGG HALF: 73 cal., 6g fat (1g sat. fat), 108mg chol., 81mg sod., 0 carb. (0 sugars, 0 fiber), 3g pro.

DEVILED EGGS WITH BACON: To mayonnaise, mix in 3 crumbled cooked bacon strips, 3 Tbsp. finely chopped red onion, 3 Tbsp. sweet pickle relish and ¼ tsp. smoked paprika.

SMOKIN' HOT DEVILED EGGS: To mayonnaise, mix in 3 finely chopped chipotle peppers in adobo sauce, 1 Tbsp. drained capers, 1 Tbsp. stone-ground mustard, ¼ tsp. salt and ¼ tsp. white pepper. Sprinkle stuffed eggs with minced fresh cilantro.

CRABBY DEVILED EGGS: Increase mayonnaise to ⅔ cup. Mix in 1 cup finely chopped imitation crabmeat, ½ cup finely chopped celery, ½ cup chopped slivered almonds, 2 Tbsp. finely chopped green pepper and ½ tsp. salt.

MEXICAN SHRIMP COCKTAIL

It's up to you how to enjoy this zippy shrimp cocktail—eat it with a spoon as a chilled soup, or use tortilla chips or crackers for scooping.
—*Erin Moreno, Arcadia, WI*

PREP: 20 min. + chilling • **MAKES:** 12 servings

2 medium tomatoes, seeded and finely chopped

1 medium onion, finely chopped

½ cup chopped fresh cilantro

1 Tbsp. grated lime zest

½ tsp. salt

1 bottle (12½ oz.) mandarin natural flavor soda

1½ cups Clamato juice

¼ cup lime juice

¼ cup ketchup

1½ lbs. peeled and deveined cooked shrimp (100-150 per lb.)

2 avocados, finely chopped
   Tortilla chips

1. In a large bowl, combine the first 5 ingredients. Stir in soda, Clamato juice, lime juice and ketchup. Add shrimp. Refrigerate, covered, at least 2 hours.

2. Just before serving, add avocados. Serve with a slotted spoon and tortilla chips.

¾ CUP: 142 cal., 5g fat (0 sat. fat), 122mg chol., 826mg sod., 11g carb. (3g sugars, 2g fiber), 14g pro.

READER RAVE

"Authentic and fresh tasting. My husband has a critical palate when it comes to Mexican food, and he gave this shrimp cocktail recipe a thumbs-up."

—LAWLER67, TASTEOFHOME.COM

HAM & CHEESE BISCUIT STACKS

These finger sandwiches are filling enough to satisfy hearty appetites. I've served the fun little stacks at every event, including holiday gatherings, showers and tailgate parties.
—*Kelly Williams, Forked River, NJ*

PREP: 1 hour • **BAKE:** 10 min. + cooling • **MAKES:** 40 appetizers

4 tubes (6 oz. each) small refrigerated flaky biscuits (5 count each)
¼ cup stone-ground mustard

ASSEMBLY
½ cup butter, softened
¼ cup chopped green onions
½ cup stone-ground mustard
¼ cup mayonnaise
¼ cup honey
10 thick slices deli ham, quartered
10 slices Swiss cheese, quartered
2½ cups shredded romaine
20 pitted ripe olives, drained and patted dry
20 pimiento-stuffed olives, drained and patted dry
40 frilled toothpicks

1. Preheat oven to 400°. Cut the biscuits in half to make half-circles; place 2 in. apart on ungreased baking sheets. Spread mustard over the tops. Bake until golden brown, 8-10 minutes. Cool completely on wire racks.

2. Mix butter and onions. In another bowl, mix mustard, mayonnaise and honey. Split each biscuit into 2 layers.

3. Spread biscuit bottoms with butter mixture; top with ham, cheese, romaine and biscuit tops. Spoon mustard mixture over tops. Thread 1 olive onto each toothpick; insert into stacks. Serve immediately.

1 APPETIZER: 121 cal., 7g fat (3g sat. fat), 16mg chol., 412mg sod., 11g carb. (2g sugars, 0 fiber), 4g pro.

⏱ SALSA ROJA

With a little help from my food processor, I can have fresh, homemade salsa ready
to enjoy in just 15 minutes. The lime juice works wonders in bringing out
all the flavors, and you can really taste the cilantro.

—Amber Massey, Argyle, TX

TAKES: 15 min. • **MAKES:** 7 cups

1 can (28 oz.) whole
   tomatoes, drained
1 can (14½ oz.) diced
   tomatoes with garlic and
   onion, drained
1 can (14½ oz.) Mexican
   stewed tomatoes, drained
1 can (10 oz.) diced tomatoes
   and green chiles, drained
1 medium onion, quartered
2 banana peppers, seeded
   and coarsely chopped
2 jalapeno peppers, seeded
   and coarsely chopped
3 garlic cloves, minced
2 tsp. salt
¼ tsp. ground cumin
½ cup minced fresh cilantro
¼ cup lime juice
2 medium ripe avocados,
   peeled and cubed
   Tortilla chips

1. Place the first 10 ingredients in a food processor; cover
and process until chopped. Add cilantro and lime juice;
cover and pulse until combined.

2. Transfer to a bowl; stir in the avocados. Serve with
tortilla chips.

¼ CUP: 42 cal., 2g fat (0 sat. fat), 0 chol., 381mg sod., 6g carb.
(3g sugars, 2g fiber), 1g pro.

DILL DIP

Be prepared—you'll likely need a double batch! One bowlful of this creamy dip is never enough at our get-togethers. It tastes great with just about any vegetable, so use whatever you have on hand for dipping.
—*Kathy Beldorth, Three Oaks, MI*

PREP: 10 min. + chilling • **MAKES:** 2 cups

1 cup mayonnaise
1 cup sour cream
2 Tbsp. dried parsley flakes
1 Tbsp. dried minced onion
2 tsp. dill weed
1½ tsp. seasoned salt
1 tsp. sugar
   Fresh vegetables or
   potato chips

In a small bowl, combine the first 7 ingredients. Chill for at least 1 hour. Serve with vegetables or potato chips.

2 TBSP.: 123 cal., 13g fat (3g sat. fat), 5mg chol., 219mg sod., 1g carb. (1g sugars, 0 fiber), 1g pro.

TEST KITCHEN TIP

For a lighter option, swap in reduced-fat mayonnaise and sour cream. Pair the dip with your favorite veggies or reduced-fat chips.

ANTIPASTO KABOBS

My husband and I met at a cooking class. We have loved creating menus and entertaining ever since. This do-ahead kabob recipe is one of our favorites.
—*Denise Hazen, Cincinnati, OH*

PREP: 35 min. + marinating • **MAKES:** 40 appetizers

1 pkg. (9 oz.) refrigerated cheese tortellini
40 pimiento-stuffed olives
40 large pitted ripe olives
¾ cup Italian salad dressing
40 thin slices pepperoni
20 thin slices hard salami, halved

1. Cook tortellini according to package directions; drain and rinse in cold water. In a large bowl, combine the tortellini, olives and salad dressing. Toss to coat; cover and refrigerate for 4 hours or overnight.

2. Drain mixture, discarding the marinade. For each appetizer, thread a pimiento-stuffed olive, a folded pepperoni slice, a tortellini, a folded salami piece and a ripe olive on a toothpick or short skewer.

1 KABOB: 66 cal., 5g fat (1g sat. fat), 9mg chol., 315mg sod., 4g carb. (0 sugars, 0 fiber), 2g pro.

⏱ LAYERED HUMMUS DIP

My love for Greece inspired me to create a fast-to-fix Mediterranean dip.
It's a delicious way to include garden-fresh veggies in your party menu.
—*Cheryl Snavely, Hagerstown, MD*

TAKES: 15 min. • **MAKES:** 12 servings

1 carton (10 oz.) hummus
¼ cup finely chopped red onion
½ cup Greek olives, chopped
2 medium tomatoes, seeded and chopped
1 large English cucumber, chopped
1 cup crumbled feta cheese
    Baked pita chips

Spread hummus into a shallow 10-in. round dish. Layer with onion, olives, tomatoes, cucumber and cheese. Refrigerate until serving. Serve with pita chips.

1 SERVING: 88 cal., 5g fat (2g sat. fat), 5mg chol., 275mg sod., 6g carb. (1g sugars, 2g fiber), 4g pro.

DIABETIC EXCHANGES: 1 fat, ½ starch.

TEST KITCHEN TIP

If time will be tight on the day of your party, chop the ingredients for this appetizer a day early and just stash them in the fridge. Then on the day of your event, you can quickly assemble the dip.

⑤ EASY SMOKED SALMON

A magazine featured this recipe years ago, and it's still my favorite salmon.
Just add crackers for a super simple yet elegant appetizer.
—*Norma Fell, Boyne City, MI*

. . . .

PREP: 10 min. + marinating • **BAKE:** 35 min. + chilling • **MAKES:** 16 servings

1   **salmon fillet (about 2 lbs.)**
2   **Tbsp. brown sugar**
2   **tsp. salt**
½   **tsp. pepper**
1   **to 2 Tbsp. liquid smoke**

1. Place salmon, skin side down, in an 11x7-in. baking pan coated with cooking spray. Sprinkle with brown sugar, salt and pepper. Drizzle with liquid smoke. Cover and refrigerate for 4-8 hours.

2. Drain salmon, discarding the liquid. Bake, uncovered, at 350° until fish flakes easily with a fork, 35-45 minutes. Cool to room temperature. Cover and refrigerate for 8 hours or overnight.

1½ OZ. COOKED SALMON: 95 cal., 5g fat (1g sat. fat), 28mg chol., 324mg sod., 2g carb. (2g sugars, 0 fiber), 10g pro.

⏱ ZIPPY CURRY DIP

Everyone eats their vegetables when this is served alongside them. The curry flavor gets stronger the longer the dip stands, so I like to make it in advance.
—*Priscilla Steffke, Wausau, WI*

TAKES: 10 min. • **MAKES:** about 1 cup

½ cup sour cream
½ cup mayonnaise
1 Tbsp. sugar
1 tsp. prepared horseradish
1 tsp. grated onion
1 tsp. cider vinegar
½ to 1 tsp. curry powder
½ tsp. garlic salt
 Assorted fresh vegetables or potato chips

In a small bowl, combine the first 8 ingredients. Refrigerate until serving. Serve with vegetables or chips.

2 TBSP.: 137 cal., 14g fat (3g sat. fat), 15mg chol., 198mg sod., 2g carb. (2g sugars, 0 fiber), 1g pro.

READER RAVE

"I made this recipe for a party recently and the guests really loved it. The key is to let the dip chill overnight (at least 8 hours). Apples are my favorite dippers."

—MIACAT9, TASTEOFHOME.COM

SHRIMP & CUCUMBER CANAPES

These cute seafood canapes really stand out on an appetizer buffet.
Tasty, cool and crunchy, they come together in a snap.
—*Ashley Nochlin, Port St. Lucie, FL*

TAKES: 25 min. • **MAKES:** 2 dozen

½ cup ketchup
4 tsp. Creole seasoning, divided
1 Tbsp. finely chopped onion
1 Tbsp. finely chopped green pepper
1 Tbsp. finely chopped celery
¼ tsp. hot pepper sauce
1 pkg. (8 oz.) cream cheese, softened
24 English cucumber slices
24 peeled and deveined cooked medium shrimp
2 Tbsp. minced fresh parsley

1. For cocktail sauce, in a small bowl, combine the ketchup, 2 tsp. Creole seasoning, onion, green pepper, celery and pepper sauce. In another bowl, combine cream cheese and remaining Creole seasoning.

2. Spread or pipe cream cheese mixture onto cucumber slices. Top each with a shrimp and cocktail sauce. Sprinkle with parsley.

1 CANAPE: 50 cal., 3g fat (2g sat. fat), 26mg chol., 218mg sod., 2g carb. (1g sugars, 0 fiber), 3g pro.

CHILI-LIME ROASTED CHICKPEAS

Looking for a lighter snack that's still a crowd-pleaser? You've found it!
These zesty, crunchy chickpeas will have everyone happily munching.
—*Julie Ruble, Charlotte, NC*

PREP: 10 min. • **BAKE:** 40 min. + cooling • **MAKES:** 2 cups

2 cans (15 oz. each) chickpeas or garbanzo beans, rinsed, drained and patted dry
2 Tbsp. extra virgin olive oil
1 Tbsp. chili powder
2 tsp. ground cumin
1 tsp. grated lime zest
1 Tbsp. lime juice
¾ tsp. sea salt

1. Preheat oven to 400°. Line a 15x10x1-in. baking sheet with foil. Spread chickpeas in a single layer over foil, removing any loose skins. Bake until very crunchy, 40-45 minutes, stirring every 15 minutes.

2. Meanwhile, whisk together remaining ingredients. Remove chickpeas from oven; let cool 5 minutes. Drizzle with the oil mixture; shake the pan to coat. Cool completely. Store in an airtight container.

⅓ CUP: 178 cal., 8g fat (1g sat. fat), 0 chol., 463mg sod., 23g carb. (3g sugars, 6g fiber), 6g pro.

DIABETIC EXCHANGES: 1½ starch, 1½ fat.

ROSEMARY-SEA SALT VARIATION: Prepare chickpeas according to step 1 in the recipe above. Toss chickpeas with 2 Tbsp. extra virgin olive oil, 1 Tbsp. minced fresh rosemary and ½ tsp. sea salt.

LEMON-PEPPER VARIATION: Prepare the chickpeas according to step 1 in recipe above. Whisk 2 Tbsp. extra virgin olive oil, 1 tsp. grated lemon peel and 2 tsp. freshly cracked pepper. Toss chickpeas with the oil mixture. Cool completely.

GREEK VEGGIE TARTLETS

The mixture in this recipe was originally a salad I made after a trip to Greece. When my husband suggested I serve it in phyllo cups, it became my most-requested appetizer.
—*Radelle Knappenberger, Oviedo, FL*

TAKES: 25 min. • **MAKES:** 45 tartlets

3 pkg. (1.9 oz. each) frozen miniature phyllo tart shells
¾ cup finely chopped seeded peeled cucumber
¾ cup finely chopped red onion
¾ cup finely chopped seeded plum tomatoes
¾ cup finely chopped pitted Greek olives
½ cup Greek vinaigrette
¾ cup crumbled feta cheese

1. Preheat oven to 350°. Place the phyllo tart shells on two 15x10x1-in. pans. Bake until lightly browned, 7-10 minutes. Cool completely.

2. Toss vegetables and olives with vinaigrette. To serve, spoon about 1 Tbsp. mixture into each tart shell. Sprinkle with cheese.

1 TARTLET: 43 cal., 3g fat (0 sat. fat), 1mg chol., 93mg sod., 3g carb. (0 sugars, 0 fiber), 1g pro.

⏱ 5️⃣ LEMON GARLIC HUMMUS

Whipping up this smooth, creamy bean dip requires just five ingredients and 10 minutes. It's a must-have at our family get-togethers.
—*Kris Capener, Ogden, UT*

TAKES: 10 min. • **MAKES:** 1½ cups

¾ cup olive or canola oil
2 cups canned garbanzo beans or chickpeas, rinsed and drained
3 Tbsp. lemon juice
2 tsp. minced garlic
½ tsp. salt
Pita bread wedges or assorted fresh vegetables

In a food processor, combine the oil, beans, lemon juice, garlic and salt; cover and process until smooth. Transfer to a small bowl. Serve with pita wedges or vegetables.

¼ CUP: 324 cal., 29g fat (3g sat. fat), 0 chol., 309mg sod., 14g carb. (2g sugars, 3g fiber), 3g pro.

READER RAVE

"This is the exact kind of hummus I was looking for. Great garlic flavor, and the lemon juice gives it just enough zing. By far the best hummus recipe I've found!"
—SINGINSLOU86, TASTEOFHOME.COM

CILANTRO TOMATO
BRUSCHETTA, 85

SUMMER

Whether you're firing up the grill, picking from the garden or dining al fresco, summer's a time to savor! These sunny snacks will help you enjoy it all.

HOT

COLD

MINIATURE CORN DOGS

Fun-size corn dogs add a little wow factor to any get-together.
Both kids and adults love them, so expect every batch to disappear fast!
—*Deb Perry, Bluffton, IN*

PREP: 25 min. • **COOK:** 5 min./batch • **MAKES:** about 3½ dozen

1   cup all-purpose flour
2   Tbsp. cornmeal
1½ tsp. baking powder
¼   tsp. salt
     Dash onion powder
3   Tbsp. shortening
¾   cup 2% milk
1   large egg
1   pkg. (16 oz.) miniature smoked sausages
     Oil for deep-fat frying
     Spicy ketchup

1. In a small bowl, combine the flour, cornmeal, baking powder, salt and onion powder; cut in shortening until crumbly. Whisk milk and egg; stir into flour mixture just until moistened. Dip sausages into batter.

2. In a cast-iron or other heavy skillet, heat oil to 375°. Fry the sausages, a few at a time, until golden brown, 2-3 minutes. Drain on paper towels. Serve with ketchup.

1 MINI CORN DOG: 68 cal., 6g fat (1g sat. fat), 11mg chol., 136mg sod., 2g carb. (0 sugars, 0 fiber), 2g pro.

GRILLED LOADED POTATO ROUNDS

This awesome recipe is my go-to for outdoor potlucks. I prep everything beforehand, then grill and top the potato slices at the party.
—*Fay Moreland, Wichita Falls, TX*

TAKES: 30 min. • **MAKES:** 8 servings

4 large potatoes, baked and cooled
¼ cup butter, melted
¼ tsp. salt
¼ tsp. pepper
1 cup sour cream
1½ cups shredded cheddar cheese
8 bacon strips, cooked and crumbled
3 Tbsp. minced chives

1. Trim ends of potatoes. Slice potatoes into 1-in.-thick rounds. Brush with butter; sprinkle with salt and pepper. Place potatoes on grill rack, buttered side down. Grill, covered, over medium heat or broil 4 in. from heat until browned, 5-7 minutes. Brush with remaining butter; turn. Grill or broil until browned, 5-7 minutes longer.

2. Top with sour cream, cheese, bacon and chives.

2 POTATO ROUNDS: 376 cal., 22g fat (12g sat. fat), 51mg chol., 424mg sod., 34g carb. (3g sugars, 4g fiber), 12g pro.

TEST KITCHEN TIP

Serve these hearty appetizers as part of a light lunch. Paired with soup or a salad, they add a bit of comforting goodness to the middle of the day.

⏱️ 🖐️ MINI ZUCCHINI PIZZAS

Looking for low carb? This simple snack recipe is a fantastic way to satisfy your pizza cravings while skipping the usual carb-filled crust.
—Taste of Home *Test Kitchen*

TAKES: 20 min. • **MAKES:** about 2 dozen

1 large zucchini (about 11 oz.), cut diagonally into ¼-in. slices
⅛ tsp. salt
⅛ tsp. pepper
⅓ cup pizza sauce
¾ cup shredded part-skim mozzarella cheese
½ cup miniature pepperoni slices
Minced fresh basil

1. Preheat broiler. Arrange zucchini in a single layer on a greased baking sheet. Broil 3-4 in. from heat just until crisp-tender, 1-2 minutes per side.

2. Sprinkle zucchini with salt and pepper; top with sauce, cheese and pepperoni. Broil until cheese is melted, about 1 minute. Sprinkle with basil.

1 MINI PIZZA: 29 cal., 2g fat (1g sat. fat), 5mg chol., 108mg sod., 1g carb. (1g sugars, 0 fiber), 2g pro.

READER RAVE

"Great snack for game day! I simply used dried basil instead of the fresh."

—JMARTINELLI13, TASTEOFHOME.COM

HOT

SWEET GINGERED CHICKEN WINGS

I discovered these amazing wings at a class I took on cooking with honey.
Whenever I serve them at get-togethers, they're among the first foods
to disappear. I've even used this chicken as a main course.
—*Debbie Dougal, Roseville, CA*

PREP: 10 min. • **BAKE:** 1 hour • **MAKES:** 2 dozen

1 cup all-purpose flour
2 tsp. salt
2 tsp. paprika
¼ tsp. pepper
24 chicken wings
(about 5 lbs.)

SAUCE
¼ cup honey
¼ cup thawed orange juice
concentrate
½ tsp. ground ginger
Minced fresh parsley,
optional

1. Preheat oven to 350°. Line 2 baking sheets with foil; coat with cooking spray.

2. In a shallow dish, combine flour, salt, paprika and pepper. Add chicken wings, a few at a time; toss to coat. Divide wings between prepared pans. Bake 30 minutes.

3. In a small bowl, combine honey, juice concentrate and ginger; brush over chicken wings. Bake until juices run clear, 25-30 minutes.

4. Preheat broiler. Broil wings 4 in. from heat until lightly browned, 1-2 minutes. If desired, sprinkle with parsley.

1 CHICKEN WING: 134 cal., 7g fat (2g sat. fat), 29mg chol., 225mg sod., 8g carb. (4g sugars, 0 fiber), 10g pro.

⏰ 🟢 BALSAMIC-GOAT CHEESE GRILLED PLUMS

Make a statement at your summer dinner party with this simply elegant treat. Ripe plums go on the grill and then get dressed up with a balsamic reduction and a sprinkling of tangy goat cheese.
—*Ariana Abelow, Holliston, MA*

....

TAKES: 25 min. • **MAKES:** 8 servings

1 cup balsamic vinegar
2 tsp. grated lemon zest
4 medium firm plums, halved and pitted
½ cup crumbled goat cheese

1. For glaze, in a small saucepan, combine vinegar and lemon zest; bring to a boil. Cook 10-12 minutes or until mixture is thickened and reduced to about ⅓ cup (do not overcook).

2. Grill plums, covered, over medium heat 2-3 minutes on each side or until tender. Drizzle with glaze; top with goat cheese.

1 PLUM HALF WITH 2 TSP. GLAZE AND 1 TBSP. CHEESE: 58 cal., 2g fat (1g sat. fat), 9mg chol., 41mg sod., 9g carb. (8g sugars, 1g fiber), 2g pro.

DIABETIC EXCHANGES: ½ starch, ½ fat.

CHEESY MEATBALL SLIDERS

These sliders are a fun way to serve meatballs without using a slow cooker. The mini Hawaiian rolls have a hint of sweetness that really complements all the wonderful Italian seasonings.
—Taste of Home *Test Kitchen*

PREP: 1 hour • **BAKE:** 30 min. • **MAKES:** 12 servings

2 lbs. lean ground beef (90% lean)
1 cup Italian-style bread crumbs
3 Tbsp. prepared pesto
1 large egg, lightly beaten
1 jar (24 oz.) pasta sauce
1 pkg. (18 oz.) Hawaiian sweet rolls
12 slices part-skim mozzarella cheese
½ tsp. dried oregano
¼ cup melted butter
1 Tbsp. olive oil
3 garlic cloves, minced
1 tsp. Italian seasoning
½ tsp. crushed red pepper flakes
2 Tbsp. grated Parmesan cheese
1 cup shredded part-skim mozzarella cheese or shredded Italian cheese blend
Minced fresh basil

1. Preheat oven to 350°. Combine beef, bread crumbs, pesto and egg; mix lightly. Shape into 12 meatballs; place on a greased rack in a 15x10x1-in. baking pan. Bake until browned and a thermometer reads 160°, about 35 minutes. Toss meatballs with sauce; set aside.

2. Meanwhile, without separating the rolls, cut rolls horizontally in half; arrange bottom halves in a greased 13x9-in. baking dish. Place half of cheese slices over roll bottoms; sprinkle with oregano. Add meatballs and sauce. Top with remaining cheese slices and roll tops.

3. Combine butter, olive oil, garlic, Italian seasoning and red pepper flakes; brush over the rolls. Bake, covered, 20 minutes. Uncover; sprinkle with grated Parmesan and shredded mozzarella.

4. Bake, uncovered, until cheese is melted, 10-15 minutes longer. Sprinkle with basil before serving.

1 SLIDER: 514 cal., 25g fat (12g sat. fat), 120mg chol., 856mg sod., 39g carb. (15g sugars, 3g fiber), 33g pro.

❄ SLOW-COOKER CHEESE DIP

I brought this slightly spicy, meaty cheese dip to a gathering with friends, and everyone dug right in. The pork sausage provides the zip.
—*Marion Bartone, Conneaut, OH*

PREP: 15 min. • **COOK:** 4 hours • **MAKES:** 2 qt.

1 lb. ground beef
½ lb. bulk spicy pork sausage
2 lbs. cubed Velveeta
2 cans (10 oz. each) diced tomatoes and green chiles
Tortilla chip scoops, red pepper and cucumber sticks

1. In a large skillet, cook the ground beef and sausage over medium heat until no longer pink; drain. Transfer to a 3- or 4-qt. slow cooker. Stir in cheese and tomatoes.

2. Cover and cook on low for 4-5 hours or until cheese is melted, stirring occasionally. Serve with tortilla chips, red pepper and cucumber sticks.

¼ CUP: 139 cal., 10g fat (5g sat. fat), 40mg chol., 486mg sod., 3g carb. (2g sugars, 0 fiber), 8g pro.

TEST KITCHEN TIP

If you won't have a lot of time on the day of your party, make this dip ahead and freeze it. Then all you need to do is thaw it in the refrigerator overnight and reheat it in the microwave or on the stovetop.

CILANTRO TOMATO BRUSCHETTA

This is an easy tomato appetizer that my family and friends love. The ingredients meld together for a delicious hors d'oeuvre that goes well with many different menus.
—*Lisa Kane, Milwaukee, WI*

TAKES: 25 min. • **MAKES:** about 2 dozen

1 loaf (1 lb.) French bread, cut into 1-in. slices
½ cup olive oil, divided
1 Tbsp. balsamic vinegar
3 small tomatoes, seeded and chopped
¼ cup finely chopped onion
¼ cup fresh cilantro leaves, coarsely chopped
¼ tsp. salt
¼ tsp. pepper
¼ cup shredded part-skim mozzarella cheese

1. Preheat oven to 325°. Place bread slices on ungreased baking sheets; brush with ¼ cup oil. Bake until golden brown, 10-12 minutes.

2. In a small bowl, whisk together vinegar and remaining oil. Stir in tomatoes, onion, cilantro, salt and pepper.

3. To serve, spoon scant 1 Tbsp. tomato mixture onto each slice of bread. Top with cheese.

1 SLICE: 98 cal., 5g fat (1g sat. fat), 1mg chol., 147mg sod., 11g carb. (1g sugars, 1g fiber), 2g pro.

DIABETIC EXCHANGES: 1 starch, 1 fat.

SO VERY BERRY BRIE

I needed a quick contribution for a party and had some berries on hand. Combining them with warm Brie cheese made for an impressive appetizer.
—*Kristin Larson, Newton, KS*

PREP: 15 min. + standing • **BAKE:** 10 min. • **MAKES:** 8 servings

½ cup sugar

2 Tbsp. water

½ cup fresh or frozen raspberries, thawed

½ cup fresh or frozen blueberries, thawed

½ cup fresh or frozen blackberries, thawed

1 Tbsp. cornstarch

2 Tbsp. cold water

1 round (8 oz.) Brie cheese, halved horizontally

Bagel and/or baked pita chips

1. In a small saucepan, heat sugar and water until sugar is dissolved. Add berries. Bring to a boil. Reduce heat; simmer, uncovered, for 3 minutes. Combine cornstarch and cold water until smooth; gradually stir into the pan. Bring to a boil. Cook and stir for 2 minutes or until thickened. Remove from heat; let stand for 10 minutes.

2. Place the bottom half of Brie cheese in a small ungreased cast-iron or ovenproof skillet; pour ½ cup berry mixture over cheese. Top with remaining cheese and berry mixture.

3. Bake, uncovered, at 400° until cheese is softened, 8-10 minutes. Serve with chips.

1 SERVING: 160 cal., 8g fat (5g sat. fat), 28mg chol., 179mg sod., 17g carb. (14g sugars, 1g fiber), 6g pro.

HOT

❄ BARBECUE GLAZED MEATBALLS

Stock your freezer with these homemade meatballs, and you'll always have a hearty snack available. We also eat them as a main dish with rice or noodles on busy weeknights.
—*Anna Finley, Columbia, MO*

PREP: 30 min. • **BAKE:** 15 min./batch • **MAKES:** 8 dozen

2 cups quick-cooking oats
1 can (12 oz.) fat-free evaporated milk
1 small onion, finely chopped
2 tsp. garlic powder
2 tsp. chili powder
3 lbs. lean ground beef (90% lean)

SAUCE
2½ cups ketchup
1 small onion, finely chopped
⅓ cup packed brown sugar
2 tsp. liquid smoke, optional
1¼ tsp. chili powder
¾ tsp. garlic powder

1. Preheat oven to 400°. In a large bowl, combine the first 5 ingredients. Add beef; mix lightly but thoroughly. Shape into 1-in. balls.

2. Place meatballs on greased racks in shallow baking pans. Bake until cooked through, 15-20 minutes. Drain on paper towels.

3. In a Dutch oven, combine sauce ingredients. Bring to a boil over medium heat, stirring constantly. Reduce heat; simmer, uncovered, 2-3 minutes or until slightly thickened. Add meatballs; heat through, stirring gently.

FREEZE OPTION: Freeze the cooled meatball and sauce mixture in freezer containers. To use, partially thaw in refrigerator overnight. Microwave, covered, on high in a microwave-safe dish until heated through, stirring gently and adding a little water if necessary.

1 MEATBALL: 42 cal., 1g fat (0 sat. fat), 9mg chol., 93mg sod., 4g carb. (3g sugars, 0 fiber), 3g pro.

⏱ ZUCCHINI & CHEESE ROULADES

My husband enjoys this recipe so much that he always wants to help roll up the roulades!
Feel free to change up the filling—I've used feta cheese instead of Parmesan
or sun-dried tomatoes in place of the Greek olives.
—*April McKinney, Murfreesboro, TN*

. . . .

TAKES: 25 min. • **MAKES:** 2 dozen

1 cup part-skim ricotta cheese

¼ cup grated Parmesan cheese

2 Tbsp. minced fresh basil or 2 tsp. dried basil

1 Tbsp. capers, drained

1 Tbsp. chopped Greek olives

1 tsp. grated lemon zest

1 Tbsp. lemon juice

⅛ tsp. salt

⅛ tsp. pepper

4 medium zucchini

1. In a small bowl, mix the first 9 ingredients.

2. Slice zucchini lengthwise into twenty-four ⅛-in.-thick slices. On a greased grill rack, cook zucchini in batches, covered, over medium heat. Grill until tender, 2-3 minutes on each side.

3. Place 1 Tbsp. ricotta mixture on the end of each zucchini slice. Roll up and secure each with a toothpick.

1 ROULADE: 24 cal., 1g fat (1g sat. fat), 4mg chol., 58mg sod., 2g carb. (1g sugars, 0 fiber), 2g pro.

🏅 ❄ ROOT BEER PULLED PORK NACHOS

Everyone loves DIY nachos! I count on my slow cooker to do most of the work when I have a house full of summer guests. This recipe calls for root beer or cola, but feel free to substitute ginger ale or lemon-lime soda if you prefer.

—*James Schend, Pleasant Prairie, WI*

PREP: 20 min. • **COOK:** 8 hours • **MAKES:** 12 servings

1   **boneless pork shoulder butt roast (3 to 4 lbs.)**
1   **can (12 oz.) root beer or cola**
12 **cups tortilla chips**
2   **cups shredded cheddar cheese**
2   **medium tomatoes, chopped**
    Optional: Pico de gallo, chopped green onions and sliced jalapeno peppers

1. In a 4- or 5-qt. slow cooker, combine pork roast and root beer. Cook, covered, on low until meat is tender, 8-9 hours.

2. Remove pork roast; cool slightly. When cool enough to handle, shred meat with 2 forks. Return to slow cooker; keep warm.

3. To serve, drain the pork. Layer tortilla chips with pork, cheese, tomatoes and optional toppings as desired. Serve immediately.

1 SERVING: 391 cal., 23g fat (8g sat. fat), 86mg chol., 287mg sod., 20g carb. (4g sugars, 1g fiber), 25g pro.

TEST KITCHEN TIP

The cooked, cooled meat can be frozen in freezer containers for up to 4 months. Just make sure the cooking liquid covers the meat so it doesn't dry out. To use, partially thaw in the refrigerator overnight and then reheat in the microwave or on the stovetop.

GRILLED PINEAPPLE WITH LIME DIP

Serve this refreshing fruit as an appetizer or dessert—the choice is yours!
If you'd like, roll the pineapple wedges in flaked coconut before grilling.
—Taste of Home *Test Kitchen*

PREP: 20 min. + marinating • **GRILL:** 10 min. • **MAKES:** 8 servings

1   fresh pineapple
¼   cup packed brown sugar
3   Tbsp. honey
2   Tbsp. lime juice

LIME DIP

3   oz. cream cheese,
    softened
¼   cup plain yogurt
2   Tbsp. honey
1   Tbsp. brown sugar
1   Tbsp. lime juice
1   tsp. grated lime zest

1. Peel and core pineapple; cut vertically into 8 wedges. Cut each wedge horizontally into 2 spears. In a bowl or shallow dish, combine brown sugar, honey and lime juice; add the pineapple and turn to coat. Cover and refrigerate for 1 hour.

2. In a small bowl, beat the cream cheese until smooth. Beat in yogurt, honey, brown sugar, lime juice and zest. Cover and refrigerate until serving.

3. Coat the grill rack with cooking spray before starting the grill. Drain pineapple spears, discarding the marinade. Grill pineapple spears, covered, over medium heat for 3-4 minutes on each side or until grill marks are golden brown. Serve with lime dip.

2 SPEARS WITH 2 TBSP. DIP: 160 cal., 4g fat (2g sat. fat), 12mg chol., 41mg sod., 32g carb. (28g sugars, 2g fiber), 2g pro.

HEIRLOOM TOMATO GALETTE WITH PECORINO

I found beautiful heirloom tomatoes and just had to show them off.
In this simple galette, the tomatoes are tangy and the crust is beyond buttery.
—*Jessica Chang, Playa Vista, CA*

PREP: 10 min. + chilling • **BAKE:** 25 min. + cooling • **MAKES:** 6 servings

1 cup all-purpose flour
1 tsp. baking powder
¾ tsp. kosher salt, divided
½ cup cold unsalted butter, cubed
½ cup sour cream
2 cups cherry tomatoes, halved
3 oz. pecorino Romano cheese, thinly sliced

1. Whisk the flour, baking powder and ½ tsp. salt; cut in butter until mixture resembles coarse crumbs. Stir in sour cream until dough forms a ball. Shape into a disk; wrap and refrigerate until firm enough to roll, about 2 hours.

2. Meanwhile, place tomatoes in a colander; toss with remaining salt. Let stand 15 minutes.

3. Preheat oven to 425°. On a floured sheet of parchment, roll dough into a 12-in. circle. Transfer to a baking sheet.

4. Place cheese slices over crust to within 2 in. of edge; arrange tomatoes over cheese. Fold crust edges over filling, pleating as you go and leaving center uncovered. Bake until crust is golden brown and cheese is bubbly, about 25 minutes. Cool 10 minutes before slicing.

1 SLICE: 317 cal., 23g fat (15g sat. fat), 68mg chol., 559mg sod., 19g carb. (2g sugars, 1g fiber), 9g pro.

🕐 GRILLED CHICKEN, MANGO & BLUE CHEESE TORTILLAS

Here's a fantastic outdoor appetizer to kick-start your summer get-togethers.
We double or even triple the recipe when we host parties.

—Josee Lanzi, New Port Richey, FL

....

TAKES: 30 min. • **MAKES:** 16 appetizers

1   **boneless skinless chicken breast (8 oz.)**
1   **tsp. blackened seasoning**
¾   **cup plain yogurt**
1½   **tsp. grated lime zest**
2   **Tbsp. lime juice**
¼   **tsp. salt**
⅛   **tsp. pepper**
1   **cup finely chopped peeled mango**
⅓   **cup finely chopped red onion**
4   **flour tortillas (8 in.)**
½   **cup crumbled blue cheese**
2   **Tbsp. minced fresh cilantro**

1. Sprinkle the chicken with blackened seasoning. On a lightly oiled rack, grill chicken, covered, over medium heat 6-8 minutes on each side or until a thermometer reads 165°.

2. Meanwhile, in a small bowl, mix yogurt, lime zest, lime juice, salt and pepper. Cool chicken slightly; finely chop and transfer to a small bowl. Stir in mango and onion.

3. Grill the tortillas, uncovered, over medium heat 2-3 minutes or until puffed. Turn; top with the chicken mixture and cheese. Grill, covered, 2-3 minutes longer or until bottoms of tortillas are lightly browned. Drizzle with yogurt mixture; sprinkle with cilantro. Cut each tortilla into 4 wedges.

1 WEDGE: 85 cal., 3g fat (1g sat. fat), 12mg chol., 165mg sod., 10g carb. (2g sugars, 1g fiber), 5g pro.

DIABETIC EXCHANGES: 1 lean meat, ½ starch.

MINI BLTS

Savor the taste of a classic BLT sandwich in one delicious little bite.
Celery adds a nice crunch to these popular, no-fuss appetizers.
—*Elizabeth Borgemenke, Mason, OH*

PREP: 30 min. + chilling • **MAKES:** 28 appetizers

- 28 cherry tomatoes
- 7 bacon strips, cooked and crumbled
- ½ cup fat-free mayonnaise
- ⅓ cup chopped green onions
- 3 Tbsp. grated Parmesan cheese
- 2 Tbsp. finely chopped celery
- 2 Tbsp. minced fresh parsley

Cut a thin slice from the bottoms of tomatoes to allow them to rest flat. Cut a thin slice off the top of each tomato. Scoop out and discard pulp; invert tomatoes onto paper towels to drain. In a small bowl, combine the bacon, mayonnaise, onions, cheese, celery and parsley. Spoon into tomatoes. Cover and refrigerate at least 2 hours.

2 FILLED TOMATOES: 38 cal., 2g fat (1g sat. fat), 4mg chol., 144mg sod., 3g carb. (2g sugars, 1g fiber), 2g pro.

DIABETIC EXCHANGES: 1 free food

TEST KITCHEN TIP

Taking these appetizers to a party? Layer a serving platter with shredded lettuce. Nestle the stuffed tomatoes in the lettuce and cover the entire platter.

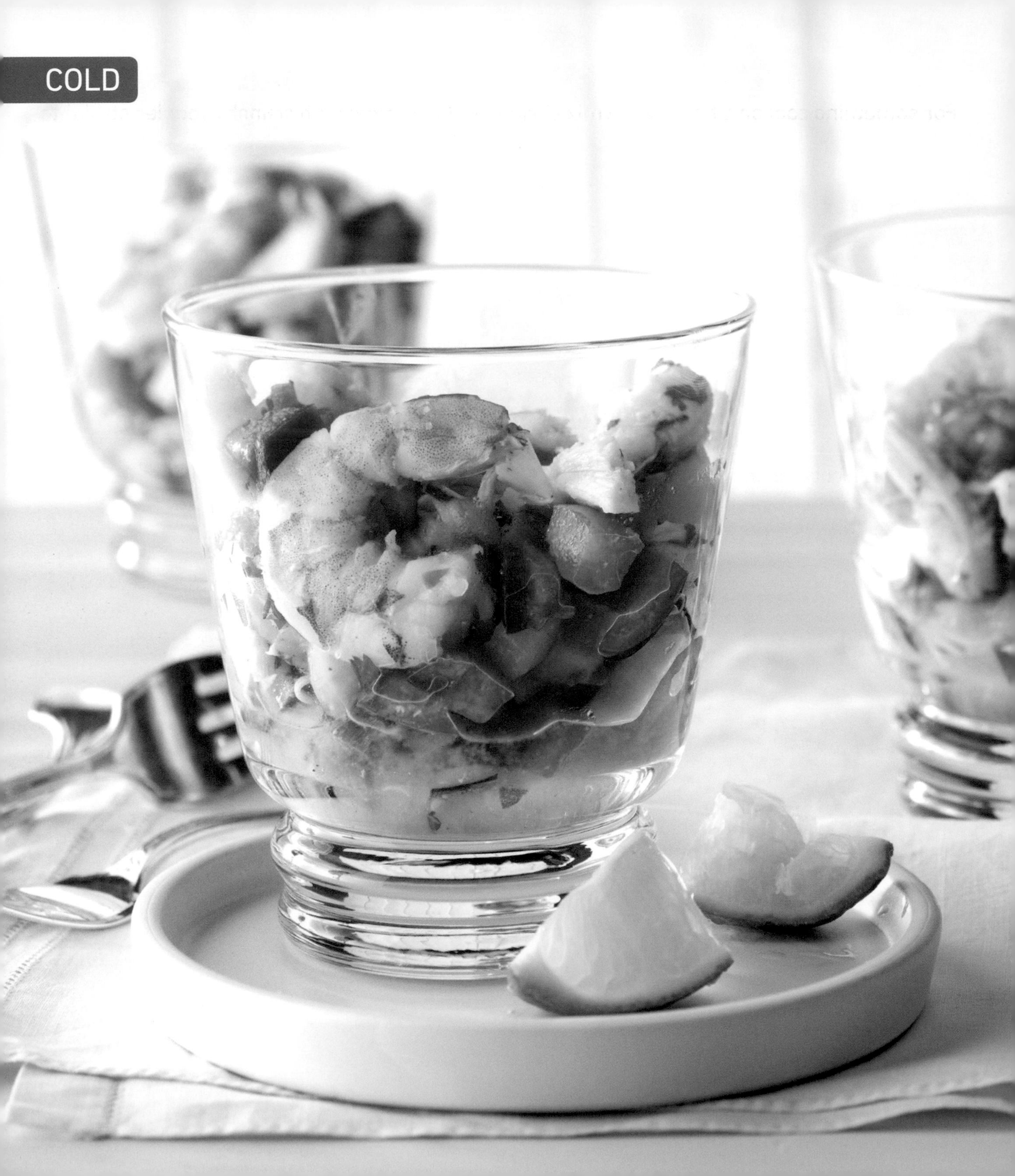

GARDEN-FRESH SEAFOOD COCKTAIL

For something cool on a hot day, we mix shrimp and crabmeat with crunchy veggies straight from the garden. Look for adobo seasoning in your grocery's international section.

—*Teri Rasey, Cadillac, MI*

PREP: 15 min. + chilling • **MAKES:** 6 cups

¾ lb. peeled and deveined cooked shrimp (31-40 per lb.), thawed
1 container (8 oz.) refrigerated jumbo lump crabmeat, drained
3 celery ribs, chopped
1 medium cucumber, peeled, seeded and chopped
1 medium sweet orange pepper, chopped
2 plum tomatoes, seeded and chopped
½ cup red onion, finely chopped
1 to 2 jalapeno peppers, seeded and finely chopped
¼ cup minced fresh cilantro
3 Tbsp. lime juice
1 Tbsp. olive oil
2¼ tsp. adobo seasoning

Combine the first 9 ingredients. Whisk together lime juice, oil and adobo seasoning; drizzle over the shrimp mixture and toss gently to coat. Refrigerate at least 1 hour, tossing gently every 20 minutes. Place shrimp mixture in cocktail glasses.

¾ CUP: 103 cal., 3g fat (0 sat. fat), 92mg chol., 619mg sod., 5g carb. (2g sugars, 1g fiber), 15g pro.

READER RAVE

"We had this as a main dish rather than an appetizer on an uncomfortably muggy evening. The seafood cocktail was refreshingly satisfying and absolutely delicious."

—ANNRMS, TASTEOFHOME.COM

HEALTHY SPINACH DIP

When I needed something light for a get-together, I came up with my own spinach dip packed with flavorful veggies. Someone requests the recipe every time I serve it.
—*Noelle Myers, Grand Forks, ND*

PREP: 15 min. + chilling • **MAKES:** 1 cup

½ cup fat-free plain yogurt
1 oz. fat-free cream cheese
2 tsp. thinly sliced green onion
2 tsp. finely chopped sweet yellow pepper
2 tsp. finely chopped sweet red pepper
2 tsp. Italian salad dressing mix
⅛ tsp. ground nutmeg
1 cup frozen leaf spinach, thawed and squeezed dry
Radishes and carrot sticks

In a small bowl, combine the first 7 ingredients; stir in the spinach. Cover and refrigerate at least 1 hour before serving. Serve with vegetables.

½ CUP: 62 cal., 0 fat (0 sat. fat), 2mg chol., 499mg sod., 9g carb. (5g sugars, 1g fiber), 6g pro.

TEST KITCHEN TIP

Love sandwiches? Use this delightful dip as a sandwich spread in place of mayo or mustard.

🕒 WATERMELON CUPS

This summery appetizer is almost too pretty to eat! Sweet watermelon cubes hold a refreshing topping that showcases cucumber, red onion and fresh herbs.
—Taste of Home *Test Kitchen*

TAKES: 25 min. • **MAKES:** 16 appetizers

16 seedless watermelon cubes (1 in.)
⅓ cup finely chopped cucumber
5 tsp. finely chopped red onion
2 tsp. minced fresh mint
2 tsp. minced fresh cilantro
½ to 1 tsp. lime juice

1. Using a small melon baller or measuring spoon, scoop out the center of each watermelon cube, leaving a ¼-in. shell (save pulp for another use).

2. In a small bowl, combine the remaining ingredients; spoon into watermelon cubes.

1 PIECE: 7 cal., 0 fat (0 sat. fat), 0 chol., 1mg sod., 2g carb. (2g sugars, 0 fiber), 0 pro.

⏱ PEACHY JALAPENO GUACAMOLE

Fresh jalapenos and ripe peaches add layers of flavor to this creamy guacamole.
It has a little kick to it without being too spicy to serve to guests.
—*Colleen Delawder, Herndon, VA*

TAKES: 15 min. • **MAKES:** 1½ cups

2   medium ripe avocados, peeled and cubed
2   Tbsp. lime juice
½   tsp. kosher salt
½   tsp. ground cumin
¼   tsp. pepper
1   medium peach, peeled and finely chopped
1   jalapeno pepper, seeded and minced
2   Tbsp. finely chopped red onion
    Tortilla chips

Mash avocados with lime juice, salt, cumin and pepper. Gently stir in peach, jalapeno and red onion. Serve with tortilla chips.

¼ CUP: 90 cal., 7g fat (1g sat. fat), 0 chol., 164mg sod., 7g carb. (2g sugars, 4g fiber), 1g pro.

DIABETIC EXCHANGES: 1 fat, ½ starch.

TEST KITCHEN TIP

We love this guacamole with chips, but it would complement grilled fish or chicken, too.

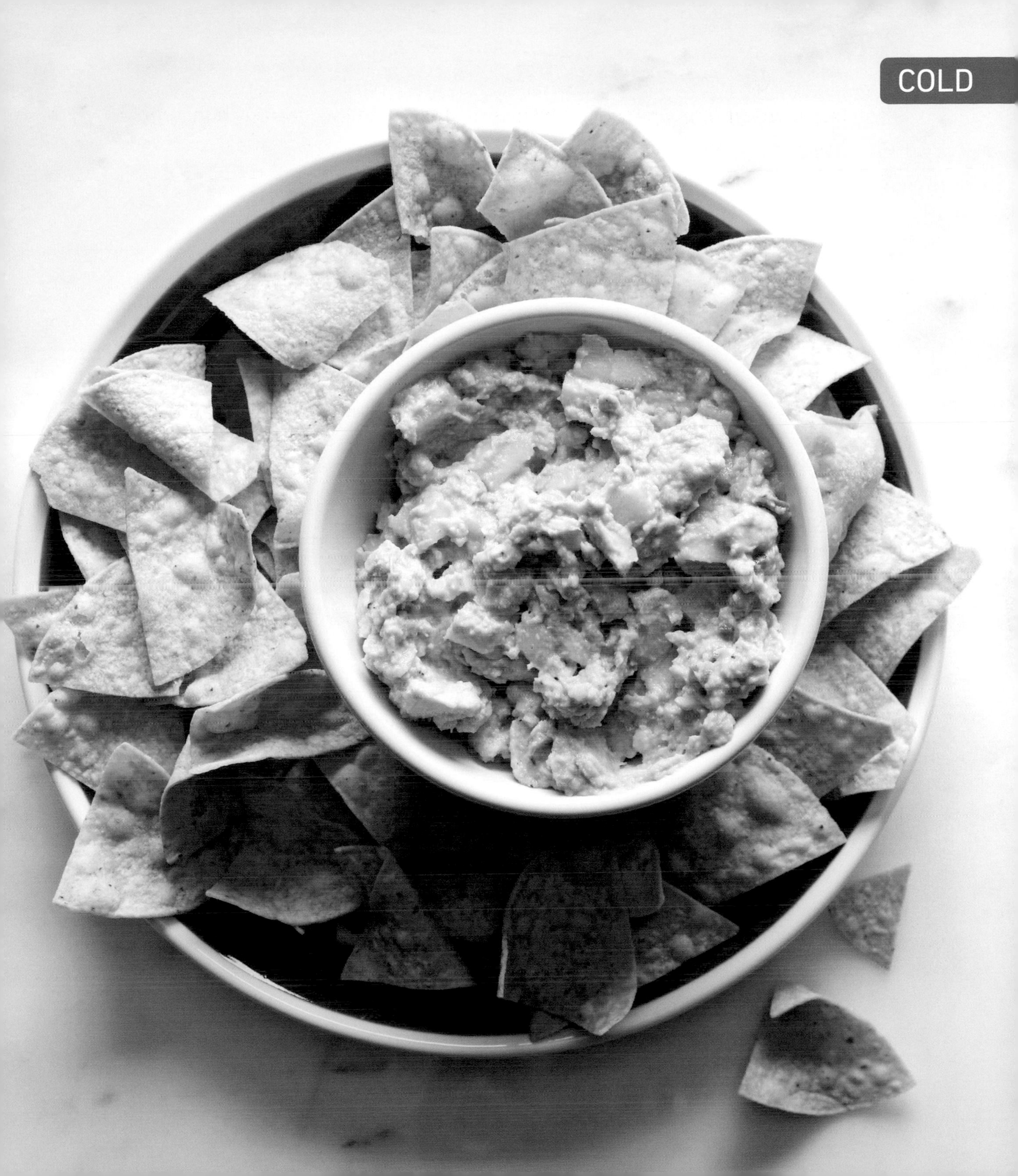

⏱ SWEET ONION PIMIENTO CHEESE DEVILED EGGS

For my mother's 92nd birthday, we had pimiento-topped deviled eggs as part of the spread. They're timeless and always in good taste.
—Linda Foreman, Locust Grove, OK

TAKES: 15 min. • **MAKES:** 1 dozen

6   hard-boiled large eggs
¼   cup finely shredded sharp cheddar cheese
2   Tbsp. mayonnaise
4   tsp. diced pimientos, drained
2   tsp. finely chopped sweet onion
1   tsp. Dijon mustard
1   small garlic clove, minced
¼   tsp. salt
⅛   tsp. pepper
     Additional diced pimientos and finely shredded sharp cheddar cheese

Cut eggs lengthwise in half. Remove yolks, reserving whites. In a bowl, mash yolks. Stir in cheese, mayonnaise, pimientos, onion, mustard, garlic, salt and pepper. Spoon or pipe mixture into egg whites. Sprinkle with additional pimientos and cheese. Refrigerate, covered, until serving.

1 STUFFED EGG HALF: 67 cal., 5g fat (2g sat. fat), 96mg chol., 128mg sod., 1g carb. (0 sugars, 0 fiber), 4g pro.

TEST KITCHEN TIP

To quickly peel fresh garlic, gently crush the clove with the flat side of a large knife blade to loosen the peel. Don't have a large knife handy? Use a small can.

AVOCADO SALSA

This chunky overnight salsa has been popular at parties since the first time I made it. Everyone loves the garlic, corn and avocado combination.

—*Susan Vandermeer, Ogden, UT*

PREP: 20 min. + chilling • **MAKES:** about 7 cups

1⅔ cups (about 8¼ oz.) frozen corn, thawed

2 cans (2¼ oz. each) sliced ripe olives, drained

1 medium sweet red pepper, chopped

1 small onion, chopped

5 garlic cloves, minced

⅓ cup olive oil

¼ cup lemon juice

3 Tbsp. cider vinegar

1 tsp. dried oregano

½ tsp. salt

½ tsp. pepper

4 medium ripe avocados, peeled

Tortilla chips

1. Combine corn, olives, red pepper and onion. In another bowl, mix the next 7 ingredients. Pour over corn mixture; toss to coat. Refrigerate, covered, overnight.

2. Just before serving, chop avocados; stir into salsa. Serve with tortilla chips.

¼ CUP: 82 cal., 7g fat (1g sat. fat), 0 chol., 85mg sod., 5g carb. (1g sugars, 2g fiber), 1g pro.

DIABETIC EXCHANGES: 1½ fat.

CREAMY RED PEPPER VEGGIE DIP

I received this, my go-to veggie dip recipe, from a college roommate.
Thick and creamy with just a touch of sweetness, it's always a winner.
—*Lynne German, Woodland Hill, CA*

PREP: 15 min. • **COOK:** 5 min. + chilling • **MAKES:** 2½ cups

2 large eggs, slightly beaten
2 Tbsp. sugar
2 Tbsp. cider vinegar
1 Tbsp. butter, softened
1 Tbsp. all-purpose flour
1 pkg. (8 oz.) cream cheese, softened
1 small sweet red pepper, chopped
4 green onions (both white and green portions), chopped
   Fresh baby carrots
   Fresh broccoli florets

In a small saucepan over low heat, whisk together the first 5 ingredients. Increase heat to medium; whisk until thickened, 4-5 minutes. Remove from heat. Stir in cream cheese, pepper and green onions; mix well. Refrigerate 2 hours; serve with carrots and broccoli.

¼ CUP: 121 cal., 10g fat (6g sat. fat), 63mg chol., 96mg sod., 5g carb. (4g sugars, 0 fiber), 3g pro.

MARINATED MOZZARELLA & TOMATO APPETIZERS

Inspired by a dish I had at a restaurant, this simply sensational combination should marinate at least three hours—the longer the better!
—*Mary Ann Lee, Clifton Park, NY*

PREP: 15 min. + marinating • **BAKE:** 5 min. • **MAKES:** 16 servings

- ½ cup Italian salad dressing
- 2 Tbsp. minced fresh basil
- 2 Tbsp. minced fresh chives
- ½ tsp. coarsely ground pepper
- 2 cartons (8 oz. each) miniature fresh mozzarella cheese balls, drained
- 2 cups cherry tomatoes
- 12 slices French bread baguette (½ in. thick), cut into quarters
- 2 tsp. olive oil
- ⅛ tsp. salt

1. Preheat oven to 450°. Combine salad dressing, basil, chives and pepper. Add mozzarella cheese and tomatoes; toss to coat. Refrigerate, covered, at least 3 hours to let flavors blend.

2. Meanwhile, toss the baguette pieces with olive oil and salt; arrange on a baking sheet. Bake until toasted, 4-5 minutes. Cool completely. Just before serving, add the toasted bread to the cheese mixture; toss to combine. If desired, thread tomatoes, cheese and bread on skewers for serving.

¼ CUP: 119 cal., 8g fat (4g sat. fat), 22mg chol., 171mg sod., 5g carb. (2g sugars, 0 fiber), 6g pro.

FRESH SHRIMP & AVOCADO NACHOS

I'm a fan of shrimp, and my family loves nachos. When I combined those favorites and added fresh avocados, the result was a cool yet satisfying snack.
—*Teri Rasey, Cadillac, MI*

PREP: 30 min. + chilling • **MAKES:** 10 servings

4 plum tomatoes, chopped
3 tomatillos, husked and chopped
4 jalapeno peppers, seeded and finely chopped
1 small onion, chopped
2 garlic cloves, minced
¼ cup minced fresh cilantro
3 Tbsp. olive oil
2 Tbsp. seasoned rice vinegar
1 Tbsp. lime juice
1½ tsp. sea salt
½ tsp. dried oregano
1 lb. peeled and deveined cooked shrimp (31-40 per lb.), coarsely chopped

TOPPING
2 medium ripe avocados, peeled and pitted, divided
½ cup sour cream
2 Tbsp. lime juice
8 cups tortilla chips
1 cup shredded lettuce

1. In a large bowl, combine the first 11 ingredients. Cover and refrigerate until chilled, at least 30 minutes. Stir in shrimp.

2. For avocado cream, mash 1 avocado with sour cream and 1 Tbsp. lime juice until smooth. Cube remaining avocado and toss with remaining lime juice.

3. To serve, arrange chips on a large platter. Top with shrimp mixture, cubed avocado, lettuce and avocado cream; serve immediately.

1 SERVING: 264 cal., 16g fat (3g sat. fat), 72mg chol., 542mg sod., 20g carb. (3g sugars, 3g fiber), 12g pro.

DID YOU KNOW?

Seasoned rice vinegar is different from regular rice vinegar. The seasoned variety contains added sugar and salt.

MUSHROOM CAPONATA

Pair this rustic appetizer with crackers or pita bread if you don't have bagel chips or a baguette. I've enjoyed the caponata as a topping on a green salad, too.
—*Julia Cotton, Chalfont, PA*

PREP: 40 min. • **COOK:** 10 min. • **MAKES:** 6 cups

2 large green peppers, chopped
1 large onion, chopped
2 Tbsp. butter, divided
2 Tbsp. olive oil, divided
2 lbs. fresh mushrooms, coarsely chopped
½ cup pitted Greek olives, chopped
¼ cup balsamic vinegar
¼ cup tomato paste
1 Tbsp. sugar
1 tsp. dried oregano
½ tsp. salt
¼ tsp. coarsely ground pepper
   Bagel chips or lightly toasted French bread baguette slices

1. In a large cast-iron or other heavy skillet, saute green peppers and onion in 1 Tbsp. butter and 1 Tbsp. oil for 10 minutes or until golden brown.

2. Add half the mushrooms and remaining butter and oil; saute until tender. Remove onion mixture and set aside. Saute remaining mushrooms until tender. Return all to the pan. Cover and simmer over medium-high heat for 2 minutes.

3. Add the olives, vinegar, tomato paste, sugar, oregano, salt and pepper. Reduce heat; simmer, uncovered, until thickened, about 10 minutes.

4. Serve warm or at room temperature with bagel chips or baguette slices.

¼ CUP: 53 cal., 3g fat (1g sat. fat), 3mg chol., 107mg sod., 6g carb. (3g sugars, 1g fiber), 2g pro.

DIABETIC EXCHANGES: ½ starch, ½ fat.

COLD

CRISP CUCUMBER SALSA

Here's a fantastic use for garden cukes—a zippy salsa with jalapeno, cilantro and garlic. You'll love the creamy-crunchy texture and super fresh flavors.

—*Charlene Skjerven, Hoople, ND*

TAKES: 20 min. • **MAKES:** 2½ cups

- **2** cups finely chopped cucumber, peeled and seeded
- **½** cup finely chopped seeded tomato
- **¼** cup chopped red onion
- **2** Tbsp. minced fresh parsley
- **1** jalapeno pepper, seeded and chopped
- **4½** tsp. minced fresh cilantro
- **1** garlic clove, minced
- **¼** cup reduced-fat sour cream
- **1½** tsp. lemon juice
- **1½** tsp. lime juice
- **¼** tsp. ground cumin
- **¼** tsp. seasoned salt
  Baked tortilla chip scoops

In a small bowl, combine the first 7 ingredients. In another bowl, combine the sour cream, lemon juice, lime juice, cumin and seasoned salt. Pour over cucumber mixture and toss gently to coat. Serve immediately with tortilla chips.

¼ CUP: 16 cal., 1g fat (0 sat. fat), 2mg chol., 44mg sod., 2g carb. (1g sugars, 0 fiber), 1g pro.

DIABETIC EXCHANGES: 1 free food.

TEST KITCHEN TIP

Don't skip seeding the cucumber. If you do, you may end up with watery salsa. To make seeding a breeze, halve cucumbers lengthwise and use a spoon to scoop out the pulpy centers.

ROASTED RED PEPPER HUMMUS

My son taught me how to make hummus, a healthier alternative to high-calorie dips.
Freshly roasted red bell peppers make this version special.
—Nancy Watson-Pistole, Shawnee, KS

PREP: 30 min. + standing • **MAKES:** 3 cups

2   **large sweet red peppers**
2   **cans (15 oz. each) garbanzo beans or chickpeas, rinsed and drained**
⅓   **cup lemon juice**
3   **Tbsp. tahini**
1   **Tbsp. olive oil**
2   **garlic cloves, peeled**
1¼   **tsp. salt**
1   **tsp. curry powder**
½   **tsp. ground coriander**
½   **tsp. ground cumin**
½   **tsp. pepper**
    Optional: Fresh vegetables, pita bread or assorted crackers

1. Broil red peppers 4 in. from the heat until skins blister, about 5 minutes. With tongs, rotate peppers a quarter turn. Broil and rotate until all sides are blistered and blackened. Immediately place peppers in a bowl; cover and let stand for 15-20 minutes.

2. Peel off and discard charred skin. Remove stems and seeds. Place peppers in a food processor. Add the beans, lemon juice, tahini, oil, garlic and seasonings; cover and process until blended.

3. Transfer to a serving bowl. Serve with vegetables, pita bread or crackers as desired.

¼ CUP: 113 cal., 5g fat (1g sat. fat), 0 chol., 339mg sod., 14g carb. (3g sugars, 4g fiber), 4g pro.

DIABETIC EXCHANGES: 1 starch, 1 fat.

EASY STRAWBERRY SALSA

Sweet with just a hint of peppery bite, my salsa makes tortilla chips disappear fast.
You could also spoon it over a main dish of grilled chicken or pork.
—Dianna Wara, Washington, IL

PREP: 20 min. + chilling • **MAKES:** 16 servings

- 3 cups chopped seeded tomatoes (about 4 large)
- 1⅓ cups chopped fresh strawberries
- ½ cup finely chopped onion (about 1 small)
- ½ cup minced fresh cilantro
- 1 to 2 jalapeno peppers, seeded and finely chopped
- ⅓ cup chopped sweet yellow or orange pepper
- ¼ cup lime juice
- ¼ cup honey
- 4 garlic cloves, minced
- 1 tsp. chili powder
  Baked tortilla chip scoops

In a large bowl, combine the first 10 ingredients. Refrigerate, covered, at least 2 hours. Serve with tortilla chips.

¼ CUP: 33 cal., 0 fat (0 sat. fat), 0 chol., 4mg sod., 8g carb. (6g sugars, 1g fiber), 1g pro.

DIABETIC EXCHANGES: ½ starch.

TEST KITCHEN TIP

Not wild about spicy foods? Simply leave out the jalapenos, reduce the cilantro or use only a dash or two of chili powder.

PICKLED MUSHROOMS FOR A CROWD

Serve tangy pickled mushrooms as an appetizer with toothpicks, alongside a steak, in a salad or as part of an antipasto platter. However you choose, you can't go wrong!
—*John Levezow, Eagan, MN*

PREP: 15 min. • **COOK:** 15 min. + chilling • **MAKES:** about 7½ dozen (6 cups mixture)

3 lbs. medium fresh mushrooms
8 cups water
2 cups sugar
2 cups white vinegar
2 cups dry red wine
3 Tbsp. bitters
1 tsp. onion powder
1 tsp. garlic salt
1 tsp. beef bouillon granules
1 bay leaf

1. In a large saucepan, combine the mushrooms and water. Bring to a boil; boil for 1 minute. Drain; return mushrooms to pan.

2. In a small saucepan, combine remaining ingredients; bring to a boil, stirring constantly. Pour over mushrooms; cool slightly.

3. Transfer the mushroom mixture to glass jars with tight-fitting lids. Cover and refrigerate at least 2 days. Just before serving, discard bay leaf.

1 PICKLED MUSHROOM: 7 cal., 0 fat (0 sat. fat), 0 chol., 5mg sod., 1g carb. (1g sugars, 0 fiber), 0 pro.

ROASTED PUMPKIN
NACHOS , 148

FALL

Gather family and friends on brisk days for special selections of harvesttime bites. In this chapter, they're ripe for the picking!

SWEET POTATO & CHORIZO CROQUETTES

Sausage and paprika add smokiness to these crispy bites. For a harvest party,
shape them into little pumpkins using pretzel sticks and cilantro leaves.
—*Nick Iverson, Denver, CO*

PREP: 55 min. + chilling • **COOK:** 5 min./batch • **MAKES:** 3 dozen

2   large sweet potatoes
    (about 12 oz. each),
    cut into 1-in. pieces
1   Tbsp. canola oil
14 oz. fresh chorizo or bulk
    spicy pork sausage
2   cups (8 oz.) queso fresco
    or shredded Mexican
    cheese blend
1   large egg
½   tsp. smoked paprika
¼   tsp. salt
¼   tsp. pepper
¾   cup panko bread crumbs
    Oil for deep-fat frying
    Pretzel sticks and fresh
    cilantro leaves

1. Preheat oven to 400°. Place the sweet potatoes on a 15x10x1-in. baking pan. Drizzle with oil; toss to coat. Roast potatoes 30-40 minutes or until tender. Meanwhile, in a large skillet, cook the chorizo over medium heat 6-8 minutes or until no longer pink. Drain and transfer to a large bowl.

2. Mash potatoes; add to chorizo. Stir in cheese, egg, paprika, salt and pepper. Refrigerate until cold, about 1 hour.

3. Shape into 1¼-in. balls. Place panko bread crumbs in a shallow bowl. Roll balls in bread crumbs to coat. In an electric skillet or a deep fryer, heat oil to 375°. Fry balls in batches 4-6 minutes or until golden brown, turning occasionally. Drain on paper towels.

4. Decorate with pretzel sticks and cilantro.

1 CROQUETTE: 110 cal., 8g fat (2g sat. fat), 19mg chol., 174mg sod., 6g carb. (2g sugars, 1g fiber), 5g pro.

MUENSTER BREAD

With a golden layer of cheese peeking out of every slice, this homemade bread is definitely worth the effort. The recipe makes a beautiful round loaf.
—Melanie Mero, Ida, MI

PREP: 20 min. + rising • **BAKE:** 40 min. + cooling • **MAKES:** 1 loaf (16 slices)

2 pkg. (¼ oz. each) active dry yeast
1 cup warm 2% milk (110° to 115°)
½ cup butter, softened
2 Tbsp. sugar
1 tsp. salt
3¼ to 3¾ cups all-purpose flour
1 large egg plus 1 large egg yolk, room temperature
4 cups shredded Muenster cheese
1 large egg white, beaten

1. In a large bowl, dissolve yeast in warm milk. Add the butter, sugar, salt and 2 cups flour; beat until smooth. Stir in enough remaining flour to form a soft dough.

2. Turn onto a floured surface; knead until smooth and elastic, 6-8 minutes. Place in a greased bowl, turning once to grease top. Cover and let rise in a warm place until doubled, about 1 hour.

3. In a large bowl, beat the egg and yolk; stir in cheese. Punch down dough; roll into a 16-in. circle.

4. Place in a greased 10-in. cast-iron skillet or 9-in. round baking pan, letting dough drape over the edges. Spoon the cheese mixture into center of dough. Gather dough up over filling in 1½-in. pleats. Gently squeeze pleats together at the top and twist to make a topknot. Let rise 10-15 minutes.

5. Brush the loaf with the egg white. Bake at 375° for 40-45 minutes. Cool on a wire rack for 20 minutes. Serve warm.

1 SLICE: 273 cal., 16g fat (9g sat. fat), 71mg chol., 399mg sod., 22g carb. (3g sugars, 1g fiber), 11g pro.

MINI CORN MUFFINS WITH SPICY CHEDDAR FILLING

I'm an Iowa gardener and I like to showcase sweet corn in my recipes.
These zippy, easy-to-eat bites are a fun change from the usual snacks.

—*Margaret Blair, Lorimor, IA*

PREP: 30 min. • **BAKE:** 25 min. • **MAKES:** 4 dozen

1½ cups all-purpose flour
1 cup cornmeal
2 tsp. sugar
¾ tsp. baking powder
½ tsp. salt
1 large egg, room temperature
¾ cup 2% milk
¼ cup canola oil
1 can (14¾ oz.) cream-style corn

FILLING
2 cups shredded cheddar cheese
1 can (4 oz.) chopped green chiles
¼ cup diced pimientos
1 tsp. chili powder
¼ tsp. hot pepper sauce

1. Preheat oven to 400°. In a large bowl, whisk the first 5 ingredients. In another bowl, whisk egg, milk and oil until blended. Add to the flour mixture; stir just until moistened. Fold in corn.

2. Fill greased mini muffin cups three-fourths full. Bake 15-18 minutes or until a toothpick inserted in the center comes out clean. Cool 5 minutes before removing from pans to wire racks. Reduce oven setting to 350°.

3. Meanwhile, in a large bowl, combine filling ingredients. Using a small melon baller, scoop out the center of each muffin; spoon a rounded teaspoon of filling into the center. Bake 10-12 minutes or until cheese is melted.

1 MUFFIN: 67 cal., 3g fat (1g sat. fat), 9mg chol., 100mg sod., 8g carb. (1g sugars, 0 fiber), 2g pro.

CRANBERRY SAUCE MEATBALLS

Cranberry sauce isn't just for turkey anymore! Combined with a few other ingredients, the Thanksgiving staple makes a perfect meatball topper.

—Tammy Neubauer, Ida Grove, IA

TAKES: 30 min. • **MAKES:** about 3½ dozen

2 pkg. (22 oz. each) frozen fully cooked Angus beef meatballs
1 can (14 oz.) jellied cranberry sauce
1 cup ketchup
3 Tbsp. brown sugar
1 Tbsp. lemon juice

1. Prepare meatballs according to package directions.

2. In a large skillet, cook and stir remaining ingredients over medium heat until blended. Stir in the meatballs; heat through.

1 MEATBALL: 100 cal., 6g fat (3g sat. fat), 16mg chol., 266mg sod., 7g carb. (5g sugars, 0 fiber), 4g pro.

TEST KITCHEN TIP

Try this recipe with packaged turkey meatballs, or use meatballs you've prepared from scratch.

MOROCCAN STUFFED MUSHROOMS

Coriander and cumin give the familiar stuffed mushrooms a zesty update.
The addition of couscous makes them filling, too.
—Raymonde Bourgeois, Swastika, ON

PREP: 45 min. • **BAKE:** 10 min. • **MAKES:** 2 dozen

- 24 medium fresh mushrooms
- ½ cup chopped onion
- ⅓ cup finely shredded carrot
- 1 tsp. canola oil
- 1 garlic clove, minced
- ½ tsp. salt
- ½ tsp. ground cumin
- ¼ tsp. ground coriander
- ¾ cup vegetable broth
- 2 Tbsp. dried currants
- ½ cup uncooked couscous
- 2 Tbsp. minced fresh parsley
- 2 Tbsp. minced fresh mint

1. Remove the stems from mushrooms and finely chop stems; set caps aside. In a large nonstick skillet, saute the onion, carrot and chopped stems in oil until crisp-tender.

2. Add the garlic, salt, cumin and coriander. Cook and stir for 1 minute. Add broth and currants; bring to a boil. Stir in couscous. Remove from the heat; cover and let stand for 5-10 minutes or until the broth is absorbed. Fluff with a fork. Stir in parsley and mint. Stuff into mushroom caps.

3. Place stuffed mushrooms on a baking sheet. Bake at 400° until mushrooms are tender, 10-15 minutes.

1 STUFFED MUSHROOM: 25 cal., 0 fat (0 sat. fat), 0 chol., 81mg sod., 5g carb. (1g sugars, 1g fiber), 1g pro.

HOT

MAPLE, FENNEL & SQUASH BITES

I can't stop nibbling these flaky squares loaded with harvesttime ingredients. Using convenient frozen puff pastry simplifies the prep work.
—*Lauren Knoelke, Des Moines, IA*

PREP: 35 min. + chilling • **BAKE:** 15 min. • **MAKES:** 2 dozen

2 Tbsp. butter, divided
2 cups finely cubed peeled butternut squash
6 Tbsp. maple syrup, divided
1 fennel bulb, quartered and thinly sliced
½ tsp. salt
1 pkg. (17.3 oz.) frozen puff pastry, thawed
1 large egg
1 Tbsp. water
¾ cup crumbled goat cheese
4 bacon strips, cooked and crumbled
Minced fresh thyme, optional

1. Preheat oven to 400°. In a large skillet, heat 1 Tbsp. butter over medium-high heat. Add squash and 3 Tbsp. maple syrup; cook and stir 6-8 minutes or until tender and caramelized. Remove squash; heat remaining butter in skillet. Add fennel and remaining maple syrup; cook and stir 6-8 minutes until tender and caramelized. Return the squash to the skillet; stir in salt. Remove from heat; refrigerate until cool.

2. Unfold puff pastry sheets. In a small bowl, whisk egg and water; brush over pastry. Cut each pastry sheet into 12 pieces; place on parchment-lined baking sheets. Spoon 1 Tbsp. fennel mixture onto center of each piece. Sprinkle with cheese and bacon. Bake 15-18 minutes or until golden brown, rotating baking sheets halfway through cooking. If desired, top with fresh thyme.

1 APPETIZER: 150 cal., 8g fat (3g sat. fat), 16mg chol., 174mg sod., 17g carb. (4g sugars, 2g fiber), 3g pro.

PUMPKIN HUSH PUPPY MEATBALLS

My Italian husband enjoys different kinds of meatballs, and I'm big on pumpkin. When I decided to combine our two favorites, we both loved the result.
—*Paula Marchesi, Lenhartsville, PA*

PREP: 30 min. • **COOK:** 40 min. • **MAKES:** about 4 dozen

1½ cups yellow cornmeal
1½ cups all-purpose flour
2¼ tsp. baking powder
1½ tsp. salt
¼   tsp. cayenne pepper
1   can (15 oz.) pumpkin
2   green onions, sliced
1   Tbsp. seeded jalapeno pepper, minced
1½ lbs. bulk Italian sausage
2   cups shredded Monterey Jack cheese
1   pkg. (8 oz.) cream cheese, cubed and softened
    Jalapeno pepper jelly

1. Preheat oven to 375°. Whisk together the first 5 ingredients. Stir in pumpkin, green onions and jalapeno. Add sausage, Monterey Jack cheese and cream cheese; mix lightly but thoroughly.

2. With wet hands, shape mixture into 1½-in. balls. Place on parchment-lined 15x10x1-in. pans.

3. Bake until cooked through, 40-45 minutes, rotating pans halfway.

4. Serve with pepper jelly.

1 MEATBALL: 113 cal., 7g fat (3g sat. fat), 19mg chol., 248mg sod., 8g carb. (1g sugars, 1g fiber), 4g pro.›

MAPLE PULLED PORK BUNS

Maple syrup is my sweet secret to these irresistible buns. Slow-cooking the flavor-packed pork couldn't be easier, and they're quick to roll up.
—*Rashanda Cobbins, Milwaukee, WI*

PREP: 25 min. + rising • **COOK:** 5½ hours • **MAKES:** 16 servings

1 boneless pork shoulder butt roast (2½ lbs.)
1½ tsp. ground mustard
1 tsp. salt
½ tsp. cayenne pepper
½ tsp. ground ginger
1 cup thinly sliced onion
2 garlic cloves, peeled
1 cup maple syrup, divided
½ cup water
3 Tbsp. cider vinegar
2 loaves (1 lb. each) frozen bread dough, thawed
1 cup barbecue sauce
1 cup shredded pepper jack cheese
Chopped green onions and crushed red pepper flakes

1. Season pork with mustard, salt, cayenne pepper and ginger; place in a 4-qt. slow cooker. Top with onion and garlic; pour in ½ cup maple syrup, water and cider vinegar. Cook, covered, on low until the meat is tender, 5-7 hours. Shred meat with 2 forks; discard cooking liquid and vegetables.

2. On a lightly floured surface, roll 1 loaf of dough into a 16x10-in. rectangle. Combine barbecue sauce with remaining syrup; brush ¼ cup sauce mixture to within ½ in. of dough edges. Top with half of pork. Roll up jelly-roll style, starting with a long side; pinch seam to seal. Cut crosswise into 8 slices. Place in a 9-in. pie plate, cut side down. Repeat with remaining dough and additional pie plate. Cover with kitchen towels; let rise in a warm place until doubled, about 1 hour. Reserve remaining sauce mixture. Preheat oven to 400°.

3. Bake until golden brown, about 20 minutes. Sprinkle with cheese and bake until melted, 5-10 minutes longer. Serve with reserved sauce mixture; sprinkle with green onions and red pepper flakes.

1 BUN: 358 cal., 12g fat (4g sat. fat), 50mg chol., 727mg sod., 41g carb. (14g sugars, 2g fiber), 20g pro.

ROASTED PUMPKIN NACHOS

I used to make these with corn off the cob in summer. When I wanted something seasonal for fall, I replaced the corn with roasted pumpkin. Yum!
—Lesle Harwood, Douglassville, PA

PREP: 40 min. • **BAKE:** 10 min. • **MAKES:** 12 servings

4 cups cubed fresh pumpkin or butternut squash (about 1 lb.)
2 Tbsp. olive oil
¼ tsp. salt
⅛ tsp. pepper
1 pkg. (13 oz.) tortilla chips
1 can (15 oz.) black beans, rinsed and drained
1 jar (16 oz.) salsa
3 cups shredded Mexican cheese blend
   Optional toppings: Minced fresh cilantro, sliced green onions and hot pepper sauce

1. Preheat oven to 400°. Place the pumpkin in a greased 15x10x1-in. baking pan. Drizzle with olive oil; sprinkle with salt and pepper. Toss to coat. Roast until tender, 25-30 minutes, stirring occasionally.

2. Reduce oven setting to 350°. On a greased 15x10x1-in. baking pan, layer half each of the chips, beans, pumpkin, salsa and cheese. Repeat layers. Bake until cheese is melted, 8-10 minutes. Add the toppings of your choice; serve immediately.

1 SERVING: 347 cal., 18g fat (6g sat. fat), 25mg chol., 559mg sod., 36g carb. (3g sugars, 4g fiber), 10g pro.

TEST KITCHEN TIP

Take advantage of the pumpkin in these nachos to give them even more flavor. Add a dash of rosemary, cumin, thyme or even cayenne pepper to the pumpkin before roasting it.

HOT

⑤ CRANBERRY BRIE PECAN PINWHEELS

My family always requests these during the holidays. A twist on baked Brie,
the pastries are scrumptious and make our kitchen smell amazing.
—*Jacquie Franklin, Hot Springs, MT*

PREP: 20 min. • **BAKE:** 15 min. • **MAKES:** about 2 dozen

1   lb. Brie cheese, rind removed
1   pkg. (17.3 oz.) frozen puff pastry, thawed
⅔   cup whole-berry cranberry sauce
1   large egg
1   Tbsp. water
½   cup chopped pecans

1. Preheat oven to 400°. Beat trimmed Brie on medium until smooth and creamy, about 5 minutes.

2. On a lightly floured surface, unfold 1 sheet puff pastry; spread half the Brie to within ½ in. of edges. Spread half the cranberry sauce over Brie. Starting with a short side, roll up jelly-roll style. Cut crosswise into 12 slices. Place pastries on parchment-lined baking sheets. Whisk egg with water; brush over slices. Sprinkle with chopped pecans. Repeat with remaining puff pastry. Bake until golden brown, 15-20 minutes.

1 PASTRY: 193 cal., 13g fat (5g sat. fat), 27mg chol., 193mg sod., 15g carb. (2g sugars, 2g fiber), 6g pro.

HOT DOG MUMMIES WITH HONEY MUSTARD DIP

Wrap up an instant hit for Halloween! The accompanying mustard dip adds just the right kick to these cute, flaky mini sandwiches.
—*Jessie Sarrazin, Livingston, MT*

PREP: 25 min. • **BAKE:** 10 min. • **MAKES:** 20 appetizers (about 1 cup dip)

1 tube (8 oz.) refrigerated crescent rolls
20 miniature hot dogs
1 large egg
2 tsp. water
Dijon mustard

DIP
½ cup mayonnaise
3 Tbsp. Dijon mustard
3 Tbsp. honey
1 Tbsp. cider vinegar
Dash hot pepper sauce

1. Separate crescent roll dough into 2 rectangles; seal seams and perforations. Cut each rectangle horizontally into 10 strips. Wrap 1 strip around each hot dog.

2. Place 1 in. apart on an ungreased baking sheet. In a small bowl, whisk egg and water; brush over tops. Bake at 375° until golden brown, 10-15 minutes. Using mustard, add eyes. In a small bowl, combine the dip ingredients; serve with mummies.

1 APPETIZER WITH 2 TSP. DIP: 128 cal., 10g fat (2g sat. fat), 18mg chol., 287mg sod., 8g carb. (4g sugars, 0 fiber), 2g pro.

READER RAVE

"I should have doubled the batch when I made these for the neighbors for our Halloween appetizer night. They loved them! These are so easy. My 4-year-old helped and can't wait to make them again next year."

—SHANNONDOBOS, TASTEOFHOME.COM

HOT

⏱ BEER & CHEDDAR FONDUE

This amazing fondue is my mom's favorite, so I make it for her birthday every year. The recipe calls for dipping with apples, radishes and breadsticks. I like to serve it with rye bread cubes and a variety of other veggies as well.
—*Amanda Wentz, Virginia Beach, VA*

TAKES: 15 min. • **MAKES:** 2 cups

4 cups shredded cheddar cheese
1 Tbsp. all-purpose flour
1 cup beer or nonalcoholic beer
3 garlic cloves, minced
1½ tsp. ground mustard
¼ tsp. coarsely ground pepper
Radishes, sliced apples and breadsticks

1. In a large bowl, combine cheese and flour. In a small saucepan, heat the beer, garlic, mustard and pepper over medium heat until bubbles form around sides of pan.

2. Reduce heat to medium-low; add a handful of cheese mixture. Stir constantly, using a figure-8 motion, until almost completely melted. Continue adding cheese mixture, 1 handful at a time, allowing cheese to almost completely melt between additions. Keep warm. Serve with radishes, sliced apples and breadsticks.

¼ CUP: 221 cal., 16g fat (12g sat. fat), 60mg chol., 341mg sod., 4g carb. (1g sugars, 0 fiber), 12g pro.

MUSHROOM & SMOKED GOUDA PUFF

Dinner guests will be impressed with this special starter course. It's so easy, yet it looks and tastes gourmet. If you'd like, serve a spicy mustard for dipping.
—*Christina Singer, Bellefontaine, OH*

PREP: 30 min. • **BAKE:** 30 min. + standing • **MAKES:** 8 servings

4½ tsp. butter
½ cup sliced fresh mushrooms
½ cup sliced baby portobello mushrooms
¼ cup chopped fresh shiitake mushrooms
1 shallot, minced
2 tsp. minced fresh thyme
¼ tsp. salt
⅛ tsp. pepper
1 sheet frozen puff pastry, thawed
½ cup shredded smoked Gouda cheese
1 large egg
2 Tbsp. water

1. Preheat oven to 350°. In a large skillet, heat the butter over medium-high heat. Add mushrooms and shallot; cook and stir until tender, about 5 minutes. Stir in thyme, salt and pepper.

2. Unfold puff pastry. Spread the mushroom mixture to within 1 in. of the edges. Sprinkle with Gouda cheese. Roll up jelly-roll style; pinch the seam and ends to seal. Place on a parchment-lined baking sheet, seam side down. In a small bowl, whisk egg and water; brush over pastry. Cut slits in top.

3. Bake until golden brown, about 30 minutes. Let stand 10 minutes before cutting.

1 SLICE: 210 cal., 13g fat (5g sat. fat), 37mg chol., 260mg sod., 19g carb. (1g sugars, 2g fiber), 5g pro.

TEST KITCHEN TIP

Feel free to experiment with a different kind of cheese. Try a sharp cheddar, a creamy provolone or even a blend of your favorites.

HOT

HOT

JACK-O'-LANTERN EMPANADAS

Halloween partygoers eat up these fun pumpkin-shaped pockets. The savory filling is perfectly spiced, and the refrigerated pie crust makes prep easy.
—*Matthew Hass, Ellison Bay, WI*

PREP: 45 min. • **BAKE:** 15 min. • **MAKES:** 2½ dozen

1   Tbsp. canola oil
½   cup frozen corn
¼   cup finely chopped onion
¼   cup finely chopped sweet
      red pepper
2   garlic cloves, minced
1   can (15 oz.) pumpkin
½   cup black beans, rinsed
      and drained
2   tsp. chili powder
¾   tsp. salt
¾   tsp. ground cumin
½   tsp. dried oregano
2   pkg. (14.1 oz. each)
      refrigerated pie crust
1   large egg
1   Tbsp. water

1. Preheat oven to 425°. In a large skillet, heat oil over medium heat. Add corn, onion and pepper; cook and stir 2-3 minutes or until tender. Add garlic; cook 1 minute longer. Stir in pumpkin, beans and seasonings; heat through. Cool slightly.

2. On a lightly floured surface, unroll the pie crust. Cut 60 pumpkins with a 3-in. floured pumpkin-shaped or round cookie cutter, rerolling crust as necessary. Place half the pumpkin cutouts 2 in. apart on parchment-lined baking sheets; top each with about 1 Tbsp. pumpkin mixture. Using a knife, cut jack-o'-lantern faces or slits out of the remaining cutouts. Place over the top of the pumpkin mixture; press edges with a fork to seal.

3. In a small bowl, whisk the egg and water; brush over the empanadas. Bake until golden brown, 12-15 minutes. Remove from pan to wire racks.

1 EMPANADA: 137 cal., 8g fat (3g sat. fat), 11mg chol., 174mg sod., 15g carb. (2g sugars, 1g fiber), 2g pro.

⏱ SWEET POTATO CROSTINI

For fall parties, I turn the classic side dish of marshmallow-topped sweet potatoes into an appetizer by serving it on French baguette slices.

—Steve Westphal, Wind Lake, WI

....

TAKES: 30 min. • **MAKES:** 2 dozen

2   Tbsp. sugar
½   tsp. ground cinnamon
24   slices French bread
     baguette (¼ in. thick)
2   to 3 Tbsp. butter, melted

TOPPING
2   cups mashed sweet
     potatoes
¼   cup chopped pecans
3   Tbsp. packed brown sugar
2   Tbsp. butter, melted
1¼   cups miniature
     marshmallows, halved

1. Preheat oven to 375°. Mix the sugar and cinnamon. Arrange baguette slices on an ungreased baking sheet. Brush with butter; sprinkle with the sugar mixture. Bake until lightly browned, 5-7 minutes. Remove from oven; preheat broiler.

2. Mix sweet potatoes, pecans, brown sugar and butter; spread over toasts. Top with marshmallows, pressing lightly. Broil 3-4 in. from heat until marshmallows are lightly toasted, 1-2 minutes.

1 SLICE: 74 cal., 3g fat (1g sat. fat), 5mg chol., 49mg sod., 12g carb. (6g sugars, 1g fiber), 1g pro.

EASY GREEK DIP

Guests always go back for seconds of this savory dip that features shrimp, feta cheese and Greek seasoning. The light orange color is fun for Halloween, too!
—*Gina Wilson, Austin, TX*

TAKES: 20 min. • **MAKES:** 2½ cups

1   can (4 oz.) small shrimp, rinsed and drained
3   Tbsp. lemon juice, divided
1   tsp. Greek seasoning
1   pkg. (8 oz.) cream cheese, cubed
¾ cup crumbled feta cheese
½ cup chopped roasted sweet red peppers, drained
1   garlic clove, peeled
1   Tbsp. minced fresh parsley
    Baked pita chips

1. In a small bowl, combine the shrimp, 1 Tbsp. lemon juice and Greek seasoning; set aside.

2. In a food processor, combine the cheeses, red peppers, garlic and remaining lemon juice; cover and process until smooth. Stir into shrimp mixture.

3. Transfer to a serving bowl. Cover and refrigerate until serving. Just before serving, stir dip and garnish with parsley. Serve with pita chips.

¼ CUP: 113 cal., 9g fat (6g sat. fat), 53mg chol., 416mg sod., 2g carb. (1g sugars, 0 fiber), 5g pro.

GENTLEMAN'S WHISKEY BACON JAM

You can slather this smoky jam on pretty much anything. It lasts only a week in the fridge, so I freeze small amounts for a quick snack with crackers later on.
—*Colleen Delawder, Herndon, VA*

PREP: 15 min. • **COOK:** 30 min. • **MAKES:** 3 cups

1½ lbs. thick-sliced bacon strips, finely chopped
8 shallots, finely chopped
1 large sweet onion, finely chopped
2 garlic cloves, minced
1 tsp. chili powder
½ tsp. paprika
¼ tsp. kosher salt
¼ tsp. pepper
½ cup whiskey
½ cup maple syrup
¼ cup balsamic vinegar
½ cup packed brown sugar
Assorted crackers

1. In a large skillet, cook the bacon over medium heat until crisp. Drain on paper towels. Discard all but 2 Tbsp. drippings. Add shallots and onion to the drippings; cook over medium heat until caramelized, stirring occasionally.

2. Stir in the garlic; cook 30 seconds. Add seasonings. Remove from the heat; stir in whiskey and maple syrup. Increase heat to high; bring to a boil and cook 3 minutes, stirring constantly. Add vinegar and brown sugar; cook another 3 minutes, continuing to stir constantly.

3. Add crumbled bacon; reduce heat to low and cook 12 minutes, stirring every few minutes. Allow jam to cool slightly. Pulse half the jam in a food processor until smooth; stir puree into the remaining jam. Serve with assorted crackers.

2 TBSP.: 112 cal., 8g fat (3g sat. fat), 10mg chol., 118mg sod., 7g carb. (5g sugars, 0 fiber), 2g pro.

GERMAN BEER CHEESE SPREAD

We love recipes inspired by our German heritage. This tangy spread is fantastic served alongside everything, including pretzels and pumpernickel or crackers and sausage. Choose your favorite beer—the flavor really comes through.

—Angela Spengler, Niceville, FL

. . . .

TAKES: 15 min. • **MAKES:** 2½ cups

1 lb. sharp cheddar cheese, cut into ½-in. cubes
1 Tbsp. Worcestershire sauce
1½ tsp. prepared mustard
1 small garlic clove, minced
¼ tsp. salt
⅛ tsp. pepper
⅔ cup German beer or nonalcoholic beer
Assorted crackers or vegetables

1. Place cheese in a food processor; pulse until finely chopped, about 1 minute. Add Worcestershire sauce, mustard, garlic, salt and pepper. Gradually add the beer while continuing to process until mixture is smooth and spreadable, about 1½ minutes.

2. Transfer to a serving bowl or gift jars. Refrigerate, covered, up to 1 week. Serve with crackers or vegetables.

2 TBSP.: 95 cal., 8g fat (5g sat. fat), 24mg chol., 187mg sod., 1g carb. (0 sugars, 0 fiber), 6g pro.

COLD

SPICY SHRIMP & CRAB COCKTAIL

This seafood starter is so good that it makes me love a food I usually don't—radishes!
The recipe also calls for spicy V8, but Zing Zang Bloody Mary Mix works just as well.
Serve the cocktail straight up, with tortilla chips or on a bed of butter lettuce.

—*Heidi Knaak, Liberty, MO*

PREP: 25 min. + chilling • **MAKES:** 12 servings (about 9 cups)

2   **medium cucumbers, peeled, seeded and chopped**

8   **radishes, halved and thinly sliced (about 2 cups)**

2   **cups spicy hot V8 juice (about 16 oz.)**

1   **cup Clamato juice**

½   **cup finely chopped red onion**

½   **cup ketchup**

5   **jalapeno peppers, seeded and finely chopped**

¼   **cup coarsely chopped fresh cilantro**

2   **garlic cloves, minced**

½   **tsp. salt**

1   **lb. peeled and deveined cooked small shrimp**

1   **lb. lump crabmeat, drained**

2   **medium ripe avocados, peeled and cubed**

Mix the first 10 ingredients. Gently fold in shrimp, crab and avocados. Refrigerate, covered, at least 2 hours or until cold. Serve in martini glasses.

¾ CUP: 162 cal., 6g fat (1g sat. fat), 91mg chol., 604mg sod., 11g carb. (6g sugars, 3g fiber), 17g pro.

READER RAVE

"Excellent for parties, this appetizer brings in many compliments and recipe requests. I used spicy Bloody Mary mix in lieu of the V8 and Clamato."

—ZINNCOOKING, TASTEOFHOME.COM

CRANBERRY JALAPENO CHEESE SPREAD

Taking the best of several different relishes and spreads I've tried before,
I came up with my own recipe. I love the sweet and spicy combination of flavors.
—*Diane Nemitz, Ludington, MI*

PREP: 25 min. + cooling • **MAKES:** 2 cups

1 cup dried cranberries
½ cup packed brown sugar
½ cup orange juice
4 tsp. chopped seeded jalapeno pepper
1 Tbsp. lemon juice
1 tsp. grated orange zest
¼ tsp. Chinese five-spice powder
1 pkg. (8 oz.) reduced-fat cream cheese
Assorted crackers or sliced sweet yellow and orange peppers

1. In a small saucepan, combine the first 7 ingredients. Bring to a boil. Reduce the heat; simmer, uncovered, for 10 minutes or until thickened. Remove from the heat; cool completely.

2. In a large bowl, beat cream cheese until fluffy. Beat in cranberry mixture until blended. Serve with crackers or sliced peppers.

2 TBSP.: 88 cal., 3g fat (2g sat. fat), 10mg chol., 63mg sod., 14g carb. (13g sugars, 0 fiber), 2g pro.

DIABETIC EXCHANGES: 1 starch, ½ fat.

🕐 FESTIVE HOLIDAY SLIDERS

These mini turkey sandwiches with cranberry sauce, horseradish and ginger keep well in the fridge. It's so convenient to have a batch on hand for holiday get-togethers.
—*Pamela Miller, Big Rapids, MI*

TAKES: 30 min. • **MAKES:** 2 dozen

1   pkg. (8 oz.) cream cheese, softened

½   cup mayonnaise

¼   cup Creole mustard

2   Tbsp. minced fresh gingerroot

1   Tbsp. grated orange zest

1½ tsp. prepared horseradish

1   cup whole-berry cranberry sauce

4   green onions, sliced

2   pkg. (12 oz. each) Hawaiian sweet rolls or 24 dinner rolls, split

1½ lbs. thinly sliced cooked turkey

1. Beat the cream cheese and mayonnaise until smooth. Beat in mustard, ginger, orange zest and horseradish. In another bowl, mix cranberry sauce and green onions.

2. Spread cream cheese mixture onto roll bottoms. Top with turkey, cranberry mixture and roll tops.

1 SLIDER: 231 cal., 10g fat (4g sat. fat), 54mg chol., 221mg sod., 22g carb. (10g sugars, 1g fiber), 13g pro.

TEST KITCHEN TIP

Lots of leftovers from Thanksgiving? These sliders are an excellent way to use extra turkey.

🕐 ⑤ DIJON-BACON DIP FOR PRETZELS

With just four ingredients that you probably already have in your kitchen,
you can whip up a zippy pretzel dip in a snap. Love horseradish?
Start with 1 or 2 teaspoons and add more to your taste.
—*Isabelle Rooney, Summerville, SC*

TAKES: 5 min. • **MAKES:** 1½ cups

1   cup mayonnaise
½   cup Dijon mustard
¼   cup bacon bits or
    crumbled cooked bacon
1   to 3 tsp. prepared
    horseradish
    Pretzels or pretzel crisps

In a small bowl, combine the mayonnaise, mustard, bacon and horseradish. Cover and chill until serving. Serve with pretzels.

2 TBSP.: 154 cal., 16g fat (2g sat. fat), 8mg chol., 428mg sod., 1g carb. (0 sugars, 0 fiber), 2g pro.

READER RAVE

"This is my go-to recipe for family and church gatherings. It is amazing! So easy to make. I have family members who need to eat gluten free, and they love this dip with corn tortilla chips."

—DECKERROAD, TASTEOFHOME.COM

SHRIMP LOVER SQUARES

During the holiday season, my family enjoys a meal of hearty appetizers while playing a board game or watching a movie. These cool shrimp squares are part of the buffet I set out every year.

—*Ardyce Piehl, Poynette, WI*

PREP: 20 min. + chilling • **MAKES:** 2 dozen

1   tube (8 oz.) refrigerated crescent rolls

1   pkg. (8 oz.) cream cheese, softened

¼   cup sour cream

½   tsp. dill weed

⅛   tsp. salt

½   cup seafood cocktail sauce

½   cup chopped green pepper

⅓   cup chopped onion

1   cup shredded Monterey Jack cheese

24 cooked medium shrimp, peeled and deveined

1. In a greased 13x9-in. baking dish, unroll crescent dough into a long rectangle; seal seams and perforations. Bake at 375° until golden brown, 10-12 minutes. Cool completely on a wire rack.

2. In a small bowl, beat the cream cheese, sour cream, dill and salt until smooth. Spread over crust. Top with the seafood sauce, green pepper, onion, cheese and shrimp. Cover and refrigerate for 1 hour. Cut into squares.

1 SQUARE: 109 cal., 7g fat (4g sat. fat), 32mg chol., 190mg sod., 5g carb. (2g sugars, 0 fiber), 5g pro.

🕐 SMOKED TROUT PATÉ

Simple to make in a food processor, this delicious paté is always a winner at parties. Feel free to replace the trout with another smoked fish.

—Judy Walle, Toledo, OH

TAKES: 15 min. • **MAKES:** 2⅔ cups

1 lb. flaked smoked trout
3 oz. reduced-fat cream cheese
½ cup half-and-half cream
1 Tbsp. horseradish sauce
1 Tbsp. lemon juice
⅛ tsp. pepper
2 tsp. minced fresh parsley
Cucumber slices
Assorted crackers

Pulse the first 7 ingredients in a food processor until blended. Refrigerate, covered, until serving. Serve with cucumber slices and assorted crackers.

2 TBSP.: 55 cal., 3g fat (1g sat. fat), 16mg chol., 174mg sod., 1g carb. (1g sugars, 0 fiber), 5g pro.

TEST KITCHEN TIP

Consider swapping the trout with smoked salmon. You could also use pita wedges or cocktail rye bread in place of the cucumber slices and crackers.

57 WALNUT & FIG GOAT CHEESE LOG

Here's an impressive spread I make using just five ingredients. The honey is optional, but I think its sweetness really complements the tang of the goat cheese.
—*Ana-Marie Correll, Hollister, CA*

PREP: 10 min. + chilling • **MAKES:** 1⅓ cups

2 logs (4 oz. each) fresh goat cheese
8 dried figs, finely chopped
½ cup finely chopped walnuts, toasted, divided
¾ tsp. pepper
1 Tbsp. honey, optional
   Assorted crackers

In a small bowl, crumble goat cheese. Stir in figs, ¼ cup walnuts, pepper and, if desired, honey. Shape mixture into a log about 6 in. long. Roll log in remaining walnuts. Refrigerate 4 hours or overnight. Serve with crackers.

2 TBSP.: 93 cal., 7g fat (2g sat. fat), 15mg chol., 92mg sod., 6g carb. (3g sugars, 1g fiber), 3g pro.

⏱ 5ɪ GREEK OLIVE TAPENADE

Welcome to an olive lover's dream! Mix olives with freshly minced garlic and parsley and a few drizzles of olive oil to have the ultimate in Mediterranean bliss.
—*Lisa Sojka, Rockport, ME*

TAKES: 25 min. • **MAKES:** 16 servings (about 2 cups)

2 cups pitted Greek olives, drained
3 garlic cloves, minced
3 Tbsp. olive oil
1½ tsp. minced fresh parsley
Toasted baguette slices

In a food processor, pulse olives with garlic until finely chopped. Add oil and parsley; pulse until combined. Serve with toasted baguette slices.

2 TBSP.: 71 cal., 7g fat (1g sat. fat), 0 chol., 277mg sod., 2g carb. (0 sugars, 0 fiber), 0 pro.

⏱ PUMPKIN HUMMUS

Traditional hummus gets an update for autumn with the addition of canned pumpkin.
A little hot pepper sauce lends just the right amount of heat.
—Taste of Home *Test Kitchen*

TAKES: 15 min. • **MAKES:** 4 cups

2   cans (15 oz. each) garbanzo beans or chickpeas, rinsed and drained
1   can (15 oz.) pumpkin
½   cup olive oil
⅓   cup tahini
5   Tbsp. lemon juice
2   tsp. hot pepper sauce
2   garlic cloves, minced
1   tsp. salt
    Baked pita chips
    Assorted fresh vegetables, optional

Place the first 8 ingredients in a food processor; cover and process until blended. Serve with pita chips and, if desired, vegetables.

¼ CUP: 173 cal., 13g fat (2g sat. fat), 0 chol., 243mg sod., 12g carb. (2g sugars, 4g fiber), 5g pro.

BLACK FOREST HAM PINWHEELS

Dried cherries are the sweet surprise alongside the savory ingredients in these delightfully different spirals. I roll up the tortillas and pop them in the fridge well before party time, and then I just slice and serve.

—Kate Dampier, Quail Valley, CA

PREP: 20 min. + chilling • **MAKES:** about 3½ dozen

1 pkg. (8 oz.) cream cheese, softened
4 tsp. minced fresh dill
1 Tbsp. lemon juice
2 tsp. Dijon mustard
Dash each salt and pepper
½ cup dried cherries, chopped
¼ cup chopped green onions
5 flour tortillas (10 in.), room temperature
½ lb. sliced deli Black Forest ham
½ lb. sliced Swiss cheese

1. In a small bowl, beat cream cheese, dill, lemon juice, mustard, salt and pepper until blended. Stir in cherries and green onions. Spread over each tortilla; layer with ham and cheese.

2. Roll up tightly; securely wrap in waxed paper. Refrigerate at least 2 hours. Cut into ½-in. slices.

1 SLICE: 78 cal., 4g fat (2g sat. fat), 13mg chol., 151mg sod., 6g carb. (2g sugars, 0 fiber), 4g pro.

DID YOU KNOW?

The intense flavor of Black Forest ham comes from the spices and salt used to dry cure it. The ham gets its name from the Black Forest area of Germany.

BRIE APPETIZERS WITH BACON-PLUM JAM

Among my friends, I'm known as the Pork Master because I love to cook just about every cut there is. These appetizers top soft, mild Brie with a sweet-sour bacon jam that has a hint of Sriracha.

—Rick Pascocello, New York, NY

. . . .

PREP: 25 min. • **COOK:** 1¼ hours • **MAKES:** 2½ dozen

1 lb. bacon strips, chopped
1 cup thinly sliced sweet onion
1 shallot, finely chopped
5 garlic cloves, minced
1 cup brewed coffee
½ cup water
¼ cup cider vinegar
¼ cup pitted dried plums, coarsely chopped
3 Tbsp. brown sugar
1 Tbsp. maple syrup
1 Tbsp. Sriracha chili sauce
½ tsp. pepper
30 slices Brie cheese (¼ in. thick)
30 slices French bread baguette (¼ in. thick), toasted

1. In a large skillet, cook bacon over medium heat until partially cooked but not crisp. Remove to paper towels with a slotted spoon; drain, reserving 1 Tbsp. drippings.

2. Add the sweet onion and shallot to the drippings; cook and stir 5 minutes. Add garlic; cook 2 minutes longer. Stir in coffee, water, vinegar, dried plums, brown sugar, maple syrup, chili sauce and pepper. Bring to a boil. Stir in bacon. Reduce heat; simmer, uncovered, 1¼-1½ hours or until liquid is syrupy, stirring occasionally. Remove from heat. Cool to room temperature.

3. Transfer mixture to a food processor; pulse until the jam reaches desired consistency. Place cheese slices on toasted baguette slices. Top each with 2 tsp. jam.

1 APPETIZER: 91 cal., 5g fat (3g sat. fat), 17mg chol., 205mg sod., 6g carb. (3g sugars, 0 fiber), 4g pro.

HAM-CHEDDAR CHEESE BALL

With the classic combo of ham and cheese, this spread is a year-round favorite at our house. For football parties, shape the mixture into a football and add strips of Swiss for the laces.

—*Michele Moore, Mooresville, IN*

PREP: 15 min. + chilling • **MAKES:** 4 cups

½ lb. thinly sliced deli ham
½ medium onion, cut into wedges
2 cups finely shredded cheddar cheese
2 pkg. (8 oz. each) cream cheese, cubed
1 cup chopped pecans
1 slice Swiss cheese
Assorted crackers

1. Place ham and onion in a food processor; pulse until finely chopped. Add cheddar cheese; pulse until blended. Add cream cheese; process until smooth.

2. Shape cheese mixture into a football; press pecans into cheese mixture. Cover and refrigerate at least 1 hour.

3. Cut Swiss cheese into strips; arrange over top for laces. Serve with crackers.

2 TBSP.: 108 cal., 10g fat (4g sat. fat), 26mg chol., 162mg sod., 1g carb. (1g sugars, 0 fiber), 4g pro.

MINI ROSEMARY-ROAST
BEEF SANDWICHES, 232

WINTER

Hot or cold, these welcoming starters take the chill
out of the air and set a festive mood for the holiday season.

⏱ 🕔 WARM FETA CHEESE DIP

We're huge fans of appetizers, and this simple baked dip is a mashup of some of our favorite ingredients. It goes so well with baguette slices or even tortilla chips.

—*Ashley Lecker, Green Bay, WI*

TAKES: 30 min. • **MAKES:** 2 cups

1 **pkg. (8 oz.) cream cheese, softened**

1½ **cups (6 oz.) crumbled feta cheese**

½ **cup chopped roasted sweet red peppers**

3 **Tbsp. minced fresh basil or 2 tsp. dried basil**

Sliced French bread baguette or tortilla chips

Preheat oven to 400°. In a small bowl, beat cream cheese, feta cheese, red peppers and basil until blended. Transfer to a greased 3-cup baking dish. Bake 25-30 minutes or until bubbly. Serve with baguette slices or chips.

NOTE: To prepare dip in a slow cooker, mix the ingredients as directed. Pour into a greased 1½-qt. slow cooker; cook, covered, on low 2-3 hours or until heated through.

¼ CUP: 155 cal., 13g fat (8g sat. fat), 42mg chol., 362mg sod., 2g carb. (1g sugars, 1g fiber), 5g pro.

READER RAVE

"I prepared this for an appetizer night I hosted, and everyone loved it. The feta adds a delicious savory kick, and the cream cheese makes the dip so rich. It was super easy, and I often have all of these ingredients on hand. I will definitely make this again!"

—SHANNONDOBOS, TASTEOFHOME.COM

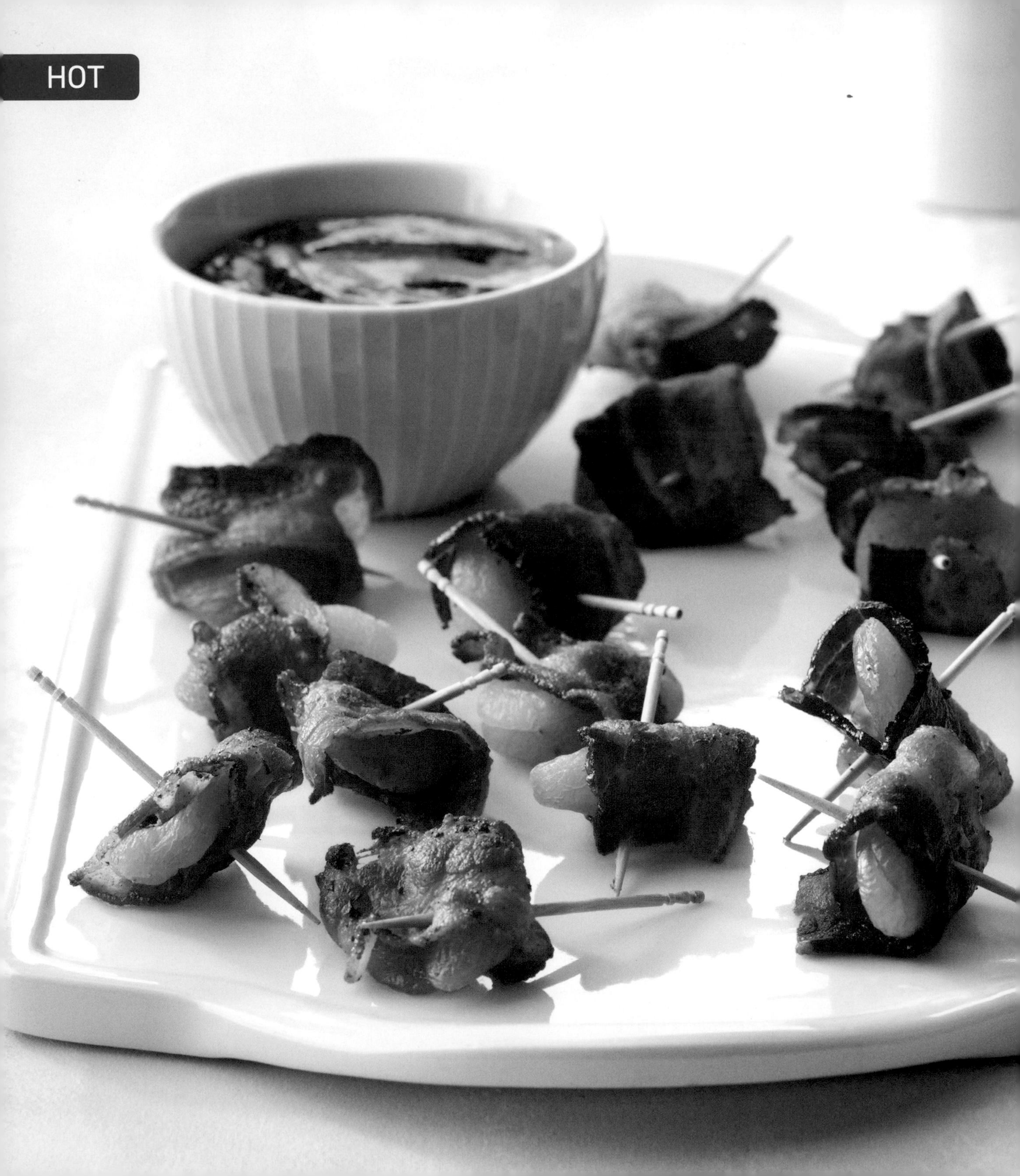

5i BACON-WRAPPED APRICOT BITES

You may want an extra batch of these sweet-smoky snacks. They're hard to stop eating!
For a variation, sprinkle on a bit of blue cheese or toasted almonds.
—*Tammie Floyd, Plano, TX*

PREP: 20 min. • **BAKE:** 20 min. • **MAKES:** about 2 dozen (⅔ cup sauce)

8 maple-flavored bacon
  strips
1 pkg. (6 oz.) dried apricots
½ cup honey barbecue sauce
1 Tbsp. honey
1½ tsp. prepared mustard

1. Cut bacon strips widthwise into thirds. In a large skillet, cook bacon over medium heat until partially cooked but not crisp. Remove to paper towels to drain.

2. Wrap a bacon piece around each apricot; secure with a toothpick. Place in an ungreased 15x10x1-in. baking pan.

3. Bake at 350° until the bacon is crisp, 18–22 minutes. Meanwhile, in a small bowl, combine barbecue sauce, honey and mustard. Serve with warm apricot bites.

1 PIECE: 47 cal., 1g fat (0 sat. fat), 3mg chol., 105mg sod., 8g carb. (6g sugars, 1g fiber), 1g pro.

TEST KITCHEN TIP

For easier cleanup, spritz your measuring spoons with a little cooking spray before measuring sticky ingredients like honey.

APPLE-PECAN BAKED BRIE

I time my fruity, spiced Brie just right so that it's in the oven as my guests start arriving. The aroma of apples and cinnamon filling the house is wonderfully welcoming.
—*Alicia Gower, Auburn, NY*

TAKES: 25 min. • **MAKES:** 10 servings

1 Tbsp. butter
1 small tart apple, peeled and sliced
⅓ cup dried cranberries
¼ cup chopped pecans
1 Tbsp. brown sugar
¼ tsp. ground cinnamon
Dash ground nutmeg
1 round (8 oz.) Brie cheese
Assorted crackers

1. Preheat oven to 375°. In a saucepan, heat butter over medium heat. Add apple, cranberries, pecans, brown sugar, cinnamon and nutmeg; cook and stir 5-7 minutes or until apple is tender.

2. Cut the Brie horizontally in half; place the bottom half in a 9-in. pie plate. Top with half of the apple mixture; replace top. Top with remaining apple mixture.

3. Bake, uncovered, 10-12 minutes or until cheese begins to melt. Serve warm with crackers.

1 SERVING: 131 cal., 9g fat (5g sat. fat), 26mg chol., 152mg sod., 8g carb. (6g sugars, 1g fiber), 5g pro.

SWISS MUSHROOM LOAF

I'm always prepared for recipe requests when I serve this irresistible stuffed loaf.
It's excellent not only as an appetizer but also as a side for pasta or chili.
—*Heidi Mellon, Waukesha, WI*

PREP: 15 min. • **BAKE:** 40 min. • **MAKES:** 12 servings

1   loaf (1 lb.) Italian bread, unsliced
1   block (8 oz.) Swiss cheese, cut into cubes
1   cup sliced fresh mushrooms
¼   cup softened butter, cubed
1   small onion, finely chopped
1½ tsp. poppy seeds
2   garlic cloves, minced
½   tsp. seasoned salt
½   tsp. ground mustard
½   tsp. lemon juice

1. Preheat oven to 350°. Cut the bread diagonally into 1-in. slices to within 1 in. of the bottom of loaf. Repeat cuts in the opposite direction. Place Swiss cheese cubes and mushrooms in cuts.

2. In a microwave-safe bowl, combine the remaining ingredients; microwave, covered, on high until the butter is melted, 30-60 seconds. Stir until blended. Spoon over the bread.

3. Wrap loaf in foil; place on a baking sheet. Bake until cheese is melted, about 40 minutes.

1 SERVING: 214 cal., 11g fat (6g sat. fat), 28mg chol., 372mg sod., 21g carb. (2g sugars, 1g fiber), 9g pro.

MINI BEEF TOURTIERES

Here's a twist on the traditional tourtiere recipe. Ground beef replaces pork, and cream cheese pastry takes the place of pie pastry. The filled mini cups make a melt-in-your-mouth addition to a holiday buffet.

—*Cheryl Bruneau, Winnipeg, MB*

PREP: 1¼ hours + chilling • **BAKE:** 15 min. • **MAKES:** about 2½ dozen

½   cup butter
4   oz. cream cheese, softened
1½ cups all-purpose flour

FILLING
1   Tbsp. canola oil
1   lb. lean ground beef (90% lean)
1   medium onion, minced
2   garlic cloves, chopped
2   Tbsp. chopped fresh parsley
1   Tbsp. Dijon mustard
1   tsp. dried savory or sage
1   tsp. poultry seasoning
½   tsp. dried thyme
½   tsp. celery salt
    Dash salt
    Dash pepper
½   cup soft bread crumbs
    Optional: Chopped tomatoes plus additional minced fresh parsley

1. Cream butter and cream cheese. Add flour, a little at a time, until a dough forms. Shape into a ball. Cover and refrigerate 1 hour.

2. Meanwhile for filling, heat oil in a large skillet over medium-high heat. Add ground beef and onion; cook, crumbling meat, until the beef is no longer pink, about 5 minutes. Add garlic; cook 1 minute more. Add the next 8 ingredients. Stir in bread crumbs to absorb meat juices. Let stand about 10 minutes.

3. On a lightly floured surface, roll out the dough to ⅛-in. thickness. Cut with a floured 2¾-in. round biscuit or cookie cutter. Press crust on the bottom and up the sides of 30 ungreased mini-muffin cups, rerolling dough as needed.

4. Preheat oven to 375°. Spoon 1 Tbsp. filling into each prepared muffin cup. Bake until crust is golden, about 15 minutes. If desired, top with tomatoes and parsley.

1 APPETIZER: 96 cal., 6g fat (3g sat. fat), 21mg chol., 128mg sod., 6g carb. (0 sugars, 0 fiber), 4g pro.

HOT

MINI PORK PIES

As a child, I discovered my love of pork pies. I used to help my father deliver oil on Saturdays, and we'd stop at a local place to have the meaty pastries for lunch.
—*Renee Murby, Johnston, RI*

PREP: 1 hour • **BAKE:** 15 min. • **MAKES:** 10 servings

1 Tbsp. cornstarch
1¼ cups reduced-sodium chicken broth
2 lbs. ground pork
3 garlic cloves, minced
1½ tsp. salt
½ tsp. pepper
⅛ to ¼ tsp. ground cloves
⅛ to ¼ tsp. ground nutmeg
⅛ tsp. cayenne pepper
4 sheets refrigerated pie crust
1 large egg
2 tsp. 2% milk

1. Preheat oven to 425°. In a small saucepan, mix the cornstarch and broth until blended; bring to a boil, stirring constantly. Cook and stir 1-2 minutes or until thickened. Remove from heat.

2. In a large skillet, cook pork, garlic and seasonings over medium heat 6-8 minutes or until pork is no longer pink, breaking up pork into crumbles; drain. Add broth mixture; cook and stir 1-2 minutes or until thickened. Cool slightly.

3. Unroll each pie crust sheet. On a work surface, roll each into a 12-in. circle. Using floured round cookie cutters, cut twenty 4-in. circles and twenty 2¾-in. circles, rerolling scraps as needed. Place the large circles in ungreased muffin cups, pressing crust on bottoms and up sides.

4. Fill each with 3 Tbsp. pork mixture. Place small circles over filling; press the edges with a fork to seal. In a small bowl, whisk egg and milk; brush over the tops. Cuts slits in crust.

5. Bake 15-20 minutes or until golden brown. Carefully remove pies to wire racks. Serve warm.

2 PIES: 561 cal., 35g fat (14g sat. fat), 94mg chol., 776mg sod., 40g carb. (3g sugars, 0 fiber), 21g pro.

BAKED BABY POTATOES WITH OLIVE PESTO

These cute little spuds pack all the appeal of a dinner baked potato into an appetizing bite. I top each one with a dollop of sour cream and coarsely ground pepper.
—*Sarah Shaikh, Mumbai, India*

PREP: 35 min. • **BAKE:** 30 min. • **MAKES:** about 3 dozen

3 lbs. baby red potatoes (1¾ in. wide, about 36)
6 Tbsp. olive oil, divided
2 tsp. salt
1½ cups pimiento-stuffed olives
½ cup chopped onion
¼ cup pine nuts, toasted
2 garlic cloves, minced
½ cup sour cream
Coarsely ground pepper, optional

1. Preheat oven to 400°. Place red potatoes in a large bowl. Add 2 Tbsp. olive oil and salt; toss to coat. Transfer to a greased 15x10x1-in. baking pan. Bake until tender, 30-35 minutes.

2. Meanwhile, place olives, onion, pine nuts and garlic in a food processor; pulse until chopped. Gradually add remaining oil; process to reach desired consistency.

3. When potatoes are cool enough to handle, cut thin slices off the bottoms to allow potatoes to sit upright. Cut an "X" in the top of each potato; squeeze sides to open tops slightly. Place on a serving platter.

4. Spoon olive pesto onto potatoes; top with sour cream. If desired, sprinkle with pepper. Serve warm.

1 APPETIZER: 88 cal., 6g fat (1g sat. fat), 1mg chol., 303mg sod., 9g carb. (1g sugars, 1g fiber), 1g pro.

DUTCH MEATBALLS (BITTERBALLEN)

I host an annual Christmas party for friends, and one year I made a dish from each person's background. What a hit! These moist meatballs with a crispy coating were a popular choice.
—*Tracey Rosato, Markham, ON*

PREP: 30 min. + chilling • **COOK:** 5 min./batch • **MAKES:** 2½ dozen

3 Tbsp. butter
3 Tbsp. all-purpose flour
½ cup beef broth
1 beef top sirloin steak (¾ lb.), cut into ½-in. cubes
¼ cup minced fresh parsley
¼ tsp. salt
¼ tsp. ground nutmeg
⅛ tsp. pepper
1⅓ cups dry bread crumbs
2 large eggs
1 tsp. 2% milk
1 tsp. canola oil
   Oil for deep-fat frying
   Stone-ground mustard, optional

1. In a large saucepan, melt butter over medium heat. Stir in flour until smooth. Gradually add broth; bring to a boil. Cook and stir for 1 minute or until thickened. Carefully add the meat and parsley; cook and stir for 2-5 minutes or until meat is no longer pink. Stir in the salt, nutmeg and pepper. Transfer to a bowl; refrigerate for 3-4 hours or until chilled.

2. Place dry bread crumbs in a small shallow bowl. In another bowl, whisk the eggs, milk and oil. Drop the meat mixture by tablespoonfuls into bread crumbs; shape into balls. Dip meatballs in egg mixture, then coat again with crumbs. In an electric skillet or a deep fryer, heat oil to 375°.

3. Fry meatballs, a few at a time, for 2-4 minutes or until golden brown on all sides. Drain on paper towels. Serve hot with mustard if desired.

1 MEATBALL: 72 cal., 5g fat (1g sat. fat), 22mg chol., 88mg sod., 4g carb. (0 sugars, 0 fiber), 4g pro.

51 SMOKY JALAPENOS

Whenever I set out a platter of these zippy snacks, every last one gets snatched up. Want to dial down the heat? Substitute mild banana peppers or yellow chili peppers.
—*Melinda Strable, Ankeny, IA*

PREP: 25 min. • **BAKE:** 30 min. • **MAKES:** 14 appetizers

14 jalapeno peppers
 4 oz. cream cheese, softened
14 miniature smoked sausages
 7 bacon strips

1. Cut a lengthwise slit in each pepper; remove seeds and membranes. Spread a teaspoonful of cream cheese into each pepper; stuff each with a sausage.

2. Cut the strips of bacon in half widthwise; cook in a microwave or skillet until partially cooked. Wrap a bacon piece around each pepper; secure with a toothpick.

3. Place in an ungreased 13x9-in. baking dish. Bake, uncovered, at 350° for 30-35 minutes or until the peppers are tender.

1 STUFFED PEPPER: 86 cal., 7g fat (3g sat. fat), 20mg chol., 215mg sod., 2g carb. (1g sugars, 0 fiber), 4g pro.

READER RAVE

"I also used some small sweet peppers for those who do not like spicy. Very yummy! Be sure to choose center-cut or higher quality bacon, otherwise these might get too greasy."

—TRACYMCELLEN, TASTEOFHOME.COM

❄ MUSHROOM BUNDLES

I love coming up with my own creations to serve as party starters.
When I tried these crispy bundles for New Year's Eve, they were gone in a flash.
—*Tina Coopman, Toronto, ON*

PREP: 30 min. • **BAKE:** 15 min. • **MAKES:** 1 dozen

1 Tbsp. olive oil
1 cup chopped fresh mushrooms
1 cup chopped baby portobello mushrooms
¼ cup finely chopped red onion
2 garlic cloves, minced
¼ tsp. dried rosemary, crushed
⅛ tsp. pepper
4 sheets phyllo dough (14x9-in. size)
3 Tbsp. butter, melted
2 Tbsp. crumbled feta cheese

1. Preheat oven to 375°. In a large skillet, heat oil over medium-high heat. Add mushrooms and onion; cook and stir 4-5 minutes or until tender. Add garlic, rosemary and pepper; cook 2 minutes longer. Remove from heat.

2. Place 1 sheet of phyllo dough on a work surface; brush with butter. (Keep remaining phyllo sheets covered with a damp towel to prevent them from drying out.) Layer with 3 additional phyllo sheets, brushing each layer. Using a sharp knife, cut the layered sheets into twelve 3-in. squares. Carefully press each stack into an ungreased mini-muffin cup.

3. Stir feta into mushroom mixture; spoon 1 Tbsp. into each phyllo cup. Form into bundles by gathering edges of phyllo squares and twisting centers to close. Brush tops with remaining butter. Bake 12-15 minutes or until golden brown. Serve warm.

FREEZE OPTION: Freeze the cooled bundles in freezer containers. To use, reheat the bundles on a greased baking sheet in a preheated 375° oven until crisp and heated through.

1 BUNDLE: 53 cal., 4g fat (2g sat. fat), 8mg chol., 50mg sod., 3g carb. (1g sugars, 0 fiber), 1g pro.

⏱ 🄯 SAUSAGE CHIVE PINWHEELS

With just three ingredients, these spirals are so easy but look special on a buffet.
Guests eagerly grab 'em—sometimes the pinwheels never even make it to their plates!
—*Gail Sykora, Menomonee Falls, WI*

TAKES: 30 min. • **MAKES:** 1 dozen

1   tube (8 oz.) refrigerated
    crescent rolls
½   lb. uncooked bulk pork
    sausage
2   Tbsp. minced chives

1. Preheat oven to 375°. Unroll the crescent dough on a lightly floured surface; press the perforations to seal. Roll into a 14x10-in. rectangle.

2. Spread sausage to within ½ in. of the edges. Sprinkle with chives. Roll up carefully jelly-roll style, starting with a long side; pinch seam to seal. Cut into 12 slices; place 1 in. apart in an ungreased 15x10x1-in. pan.

3. Bake until golden brown and the sausage is cooked through, 12-16 minutes.

1 PINWHEEL: 132 cal., 9g fat (3g sat. fat), 13mg chol., 293mg sod., 8g carb. (1g sugars, 0 fiber), 4g pro.

CRANBERRY-BEEF MINI BURGERS

Cranberry tapenade brings ruby-red color and sweet-sour zing to these fun little bacon cheeseburgers. Serve them for parties or any time you want to treat your family.
—*Priscilla Yee, Concord, CA*

PREP: 30 min. • **COOK:** 10 min./batch • **MAKES:** 16 appetizers

CRANBERRY TAPENADE
- ⅔ cup dried cranberries
- ¼ cup pitted Greek olives, chopped
- 1 Tbsp. balsamic vinegar
- 1 Tbsp. olive oil
- 1 garlic clove, minced
- 1 tsp. minced fresh rosemary
- 1 tsp. minced fresh thyme

BURGERS
- 2 lbs. ground beef
- 1 tsp. salt
- 1 tsp. pepper
- 4 slices provolone cheese, quartered
- ¾ cup mayonnaise
- 16 dinner rolls, split and toasted
- 2 cups fresh arugula
- 3 plum tomatoes, cut into 16 slices
- 8 bacon strips, halved and cooked

1. In a food processor, place first 6 ingredients; pulse until cranberries are finely chopped. Transfer to a small bowl; stir in thyme. In a large bowl, combine the beef, salt and pepper. Shape into 16 patties, about ½ in. thick.

2. In a large nonstick skillet, cook the patties in batches over medium heat for 3-4 minutes on each side or until a thermometer reads 160° and juices run clear, topping with cheese during last minute of cooking.

3. Spread mayonnaise over cut sides of rolls. Layer bottoms with arugula, tomatoes, burgers, bacon and cranberry tapenade; replace tops.

1 BURGER WITH TOPPINGS: 360 cal., 21g fat (6g sat. fat), 63mg chol., 586mg sod., 25g carb. (7g sugars, 2g fiber), 17g pro.

⑤ RISOTTO BALLS (ARANCINI)

My Italian grandma treated me to these traditional rice balls with marinara.
I still ask her to make them, and now so do my children.
—*Gretchen Whelan, San Francisco, CA*

PREP: 35 min. • **BAKE:** 25 min. • **MAKES:** about 3 dozen

1½ cups water
1 cup uncooked arborio rice
1 tsp. salt
2 large eggs, lightly beaten
⅔ cup sun-dried tomato pesto
2 cups panko bread crumbs, divided
Marinara sauce, warmed

1. Preheat oven to 375°. In a large saucepan, combine water, rice and salt; bring to a boil. Reduce heat; simmer, covered, until the liquid is absorbed and the rice is tender, 18-20 minutes. Let stand, covered, 10 minutes. Transfer to a large bowl; cool slightly. Add eggs and pesto; stir in 1 cup bread crumbs.

2. Place the remaining bread crumbs in a shallow bowl. Shape the rice mixture into 1¼-in. balls. Roll in bread crumbs, patting to help the coating adhere. Place on greased 15x10x1-in. baking pans. Bake until golden brown, 25-30 minutes. Serve with marinara sauce.

1 APPETIZER: 42 cal., 1g fat (0 sat. fat), 10mg chol., 125mg sod., 7g carb. (1g sugars, 0 fiber), 1g pro.

DIABETIC EXCHANGES: ½ starch.

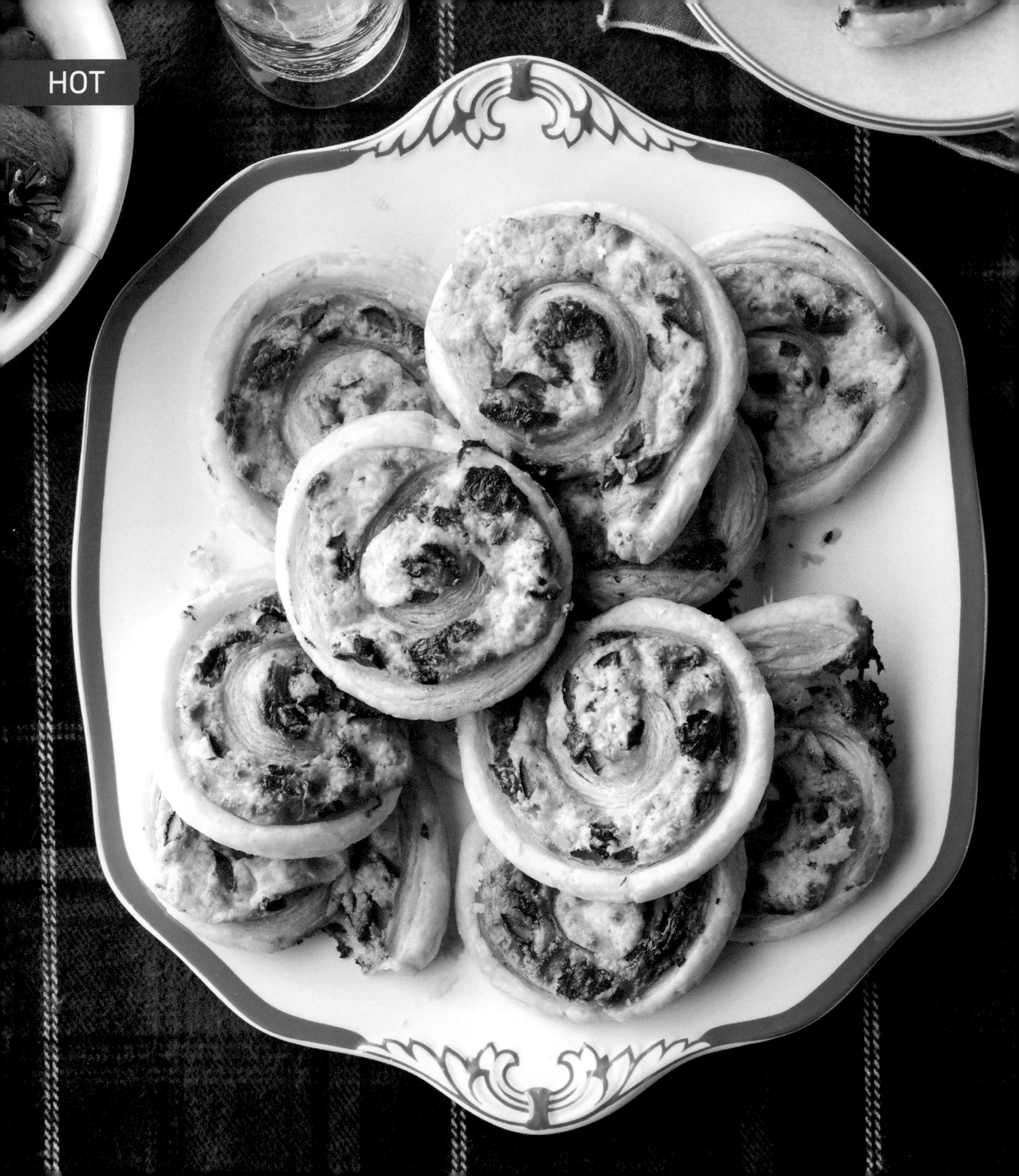

❄ MEDITERRANEAN PASTRY PINWHEELS

Sun-dried tomatoes, cheese and pesto blend beautifully in these colorful spirals.
If you make the unbaked slices ahead and freeze them, all you have to do on party day is bake.
—*Kristen Heigl, Staten Island, NY*

PREP: 20 min. + freezing • **BAKE:** 15 min. • **MAKES:** 16 appetizers

1 sheet frozen puff pastry, thawed

1 pkg. (8 oz.) cream cheese, softened

¼ cup prepared pesto

¾ cup shredded provolone cheese

½ cup chopped oil-packed sun-dried tomatoes

½ cup chopped ripe olives

¼ tsp. pepper

1. Preheat oven to 400°. Unfold puff pastry; roll and trim into a 10-in. square.

2. Beat the cream cheese and pesto until smooth; stir in the remaining ingredients. Spread cheese mixture on pastry to within ½ in. of edges. Roll up jelly-roll style. Freeze 30 minutes. Cut crosswise into 16 slices.

3. Bake cut side down on a parchment-lined baking sheet until golden brown, 12-15 minutes.

FREEZE OPTION: Cover and freeze unbaked pastry slices on waxed paper-lined baking sheets until firm. Transfer to airtight container; return to freezer. To use, preheat oven to 400°; bake pastries until golden brown, 15-20 minutes.

1 PINWHEEL: 170 cal., 13g fat (5g sat. fat), 18mg chol., 227mg sod., 11g carb. (1g sugars, 2g fiber), 4g pro.

BEST EVER STUFFED MUSHROOMS

Every Christmas Eve, I set out a platter of my fresh-from-the-oven mushrooms.
For a change, fix the yummy filling all by itself to spread on baguette slices or crackers.
—*Debby Beard, Eagle, CO*

PREP: 20 min. • **BAKE:** 15 min. • **MAKES:** 2½ dozen

- 1 lb. bulk pork sausage
- ¼ cup finely chopped onion
- 1 garlic clove, minced
- 1 pkg. (8 oz.) reduced-fat cream cheese
- ¼ cup shredded Parmesan cheese
- ⅓ cup seasoned bread crumbs
- 3 tsp. dried basil
- 1½ tsp. dried parsley flakes
- 30 large fresh mushrooms (about 1½ lbs.), stems removed
- 3 Tbsp. butter, melted

1. Preheat oven to 400°. In a large skillet, cook sausage, onion and garlic over medium heat 6-8 minutes or until sausage is no longer pink and onion is tender, breaking up sausage into crumbles; drain. Add cream cheese and Parmesan cheese; cook and stir until melted. Stir in bread crumbs, basil and parsley.

2. Meanwhile, place the mushroom caps in a greased 15x10x1-in. baking pan, removed-stem side up. Brush with butter. Spoon sausage mixture into mushroom caps. Bake, uncovered, 12-15 minutes or until the mushrooms are tender.

1 APPETIZER: 79 cal., 6g fat (3g sat. fat), 17mg chol., 167mg sod., 2g carb. (1g sugars, 0 fiber), 3g pro.

APPETIZER BLUE CHEESE LOGS

Three kinds of cheese and curry powder make this spread a little livelier than most.
Swipe it on your favorite cracker with a drizzle of honey for a sensational snack.
—*Ethel Johnson, North Saanich, BC*

PREP: 15 min. • **COOK:** 5 min. + chilling • **MAKES:** 2 cheese logs (1¼ cups)

1 **pkg. (8 oz.) cream cheese, softened**
1 **cup shredded sharp cheddar cheese**
½ **cup crumbled blue cheese**
1 **Tbsp. butter**
1½ **tsp. curry powder**
½ **cup finely chopped pecans**
2 **Tbsp. minced fresh parsley**
Assorted crackers

1. Beat cream cheese until smooth. Fold in cheddar and blue cheeses. Refrigerate, covered, at least 2 hours.

2. In a small skillet, heat butter over medium heat. Add curry powder; saute 1-2 minutes. Stir in pecans; cook and stir 1 minute. Stir in parsley. Cool slightly. Roll the cheese mixture into 2 logs, each about 5 in. long. Roll logs in pecan mixture; refrigerate. Serve with crackers.

2 TBSP.: 196 cal., 19g fat (9g sat. fat), 45mg chol., 243mg sod., 2g carb. (1g sugars, 1g fiber), 6g pro.

TEST KITCHEN TIP

This versatile recipe is fun to experiment with. For example, try swapping in Swiss cheese, finely chopped cooked ham and onion powder.

COLD

● THYME & FIG GOAT CHEESE SPREAD

When I started growing herbs in my garden, I didn't know how I would use the thyme.
This easy recipe lets that ingredient shine. I usually add a thyme sprig,
slivered almonds and chopped figs as garnishes.
—*Laura Cox, Columbia, MO*

TAKES: 15 min. • **MAKES:** 1½ cups

1   cup crumbled goat cheese
½   cup sour cream
1   Tbsp. honey
½   tsp. minced fresh thyme
½   cup chopped dried figs
¼   cup slivered almonds
    Additional minced fresh thyme, optional
    Assorted crackers, French bread baguette slices or assorted fresh vegetables

In a small bowl, beat cheese, sour cream, honey and thyme until smooth; stir in figs and almonds. Sprinkle with additional thyme if desired. Refrigerate until serving. Serve with crackers, baguette slices or vegetables.

2 TBSP.: 81 cal., 6g fat (3g sat. fat), 14mg chol., 49mg sod., 7g carb. (5g sugars, 1g fiber), 3g pro.

TEST KITCHEN TIP

If you don't have fresh thyme on hand, simply use ¼ tsp. dried thyme instead.

CHRISTMAS CHEESE BALLS

My friends and family ask for these rich cheese balls at Christmastime every year.
The simple recipe yields three that I can serve or give as gifts.
—*Margie Cadwell, Eastman, GA*

PREP: 20 min. + chilling • **MAKES:** 3 cheese balls (6 cups)

4   pkg. (8 oz. each) cream cheese, softened
4   cups shredded cheddar cheese
1   cup chopped pecans
¼   cup evaporated milk
1   can (4¼ oz.) chopped ripe olives, drained
2   garlic cloves, minced
½   tsp. salt
    Minced fresh parsley, chopped pecans and paprika
    Assorted crackers

1. In a small bowl, beat cream cheese and cheddar cheese. Stir in the pecans, milk, olives, garlic and salt. Divide into thirds; roll each into a ball.

2. Roll 1 cheese ball in parsley and 1 in pecans. Sprinkle the third with paprika. Cover and refrigerate. Remove from refrigerator 15 minutes before serving. Serve with crackers.

2 TBSP.: 125 cal., 12g fat (6g sat. fat), 29mg chol., 165mg sod., 2g carb. (1g sugars, 0 fiber), 4g pro.

Enjoy!

PUFF PASTRY HOLLY LEAVES

These elegant appetizers get rave reviews at my office holiday party. The pastry leaves look as if they require hours in the kitchen, but the prep work takes just 30 minutes.
—*Angela King, Walnut Cove, NC*

PREP: 30 min. • **BAKE:** 15 min. + cooling • **MAKES:** 2 dozen

1 pkg. (17.3 oz.) frozen puff pastry, thawed
1 large egg
1 Tbsp. water
4 oz. cream cheese, softened
1 cup crumbled feta cheese
½ cup minced fresh parsley
½ cup prepared pesto
24 pimiento pieces

1. Unfold the puff pastry sheets onto a lightly floured surface. From each sheet, cut out 12 leaves with a floured 3½-in. leaf-shaped cookie cutter. Place on ungreased baking sheets. With a toothpick, score veins in leaves. In a small bowl, beat egg and water; brush over pastry.

2. Bake at 400° for 12-14 minutes or until golden brown. Remove to wire racks to cool.

3. In a large bowl, combine the cheeses, parsley and pesto. Cut each pastry leaf in half. Spread 1 Tbsp. cheese mixture over bottom half; replace top. Add a pimiento piece on each for a holly berry. Refrigerate leftovers.

1 APPETIZER: 151 cal., 10g fat (3g sat. fat), 15mg chol., 191mg sod., 13g carb. (0 sugars, 2g fiber), 3g pro.

MINI ROSEMARY-ROAST BEEF SANDWICHES

Need something hearty? Roast beef sandwiches always go over big, especially when I dollop them with a zippy mayo mixture and add pickled giardiniera relish.
—*Susan Hein, Burlington, WI*

PREP: 25 min. + chilling • **BAKE:** 50 min. + chilling • **MAKES:** 2 dozen

1 beef top round roast (3 lbs.)

3 tsp. kosher salt

2 tsp. crushed dried rosemary

2 Tbsp. olive oil, divided

2 tsp. pepper

2 cups mild giardiniera, drained

1 cup reduced-fat mayonnaise

2 Tbsp. stone-ground mustard

1 to 2 Tbsp. prepared horseradish

24 Hawaiian sweet rolls, split

1. Sprinkle roast with salt and rosemary. Cover and refrigerate at least 8 hours or up to 24 hours.

2. Preheat oven to 325°. Uncover roast and pat dry. Rub roast with 1 Tbsp. oil; sprinkle with pepper. In a large cast-iron or other ovenproof skillet, heat remaining oil over medium-high heat. Brown roast on both sides.

3. Transfer to oven; roast until a thermometer reads 135° for medium-rare, 50-60 minutes. (Temperature of roast will continue to rise about 10° upon standing.) Remove roast from skillet; let stand 1 hour. Refrigerate, covered, at least 2 hours, until cold.

4. Place giardiniera in a food processor; pulse until finely chopped. In a small bowl, mix mayonnaise, mustard and horseradish.

5. To serve, thinly slice the cold beef. Serve on rolls with mayonnaise mixture and giardiniera.

1 MINI SANDWICH: 220 cal., 9g fat (3g sat. fat), 50mg chol., 466mg sod., 18g carb. (7g sugars, 1g fiber), 17g pro.

COLD

CALIENTE CHRISTMAS CHEESE CRISPS

Fire up the crowd with homemade crackers featuring bacon, cumin and french-fried onions. The crisps are especially good dipped in pico de gallo or picante sauce.

—*Jeanne Holt, Mendota Heights, MN*

PREP: 25 min. • **BAKE:** 15 min. • **MAKES:** 10 servings (3½ dozen)

¾ cup shredded extra sharp cheddar cheese

⅓ cup shredded pepper jack cheese

½ cup butter, softened

¼ tsp. garlic pepper blend

¼ tsp. ground cumin

⅛ tsp. salt

1 cup all-purpose flour

⅔ cup crispy brown rice cereal

¼ cup finely crumbled cooked bacon

¼ cup salted pumpkin seeds

¼ cup crumbled french-fried onions

Optional: Pico de gallo or picante sauce

1. Preheat oven to 350°. Beat the first 6 ingredients together until blended. Add the flour; mix until a dough forms. Stir in remaining ingredients except optional sauce.

2. Shape dough into 1-in. balls. Place on ungreased baking sheets; flatten with a lightly floured glass.

3. Bake until golden, 14-16 minutes. Remove to wire racks; cool completely. If desired, serve crisps with pico de gallo or picante sauce.

4 CRISPS: 217 cal., 16g fat (9g sat. fat), 37mg chol., 249mg sod., 13g carb. (0 sugars, 1g fiber), 6g pro.

CRANBERRY CREAM CHEESE SPREAD

Take 10 minutes to blend four ingredients, and you'll have a yummy spread for the holidays. It has a hint of sweetness that appeals to children and adults alike.
—*Frankie Robinson, Lockhart, TX*

TAKES: 10 min. • **MAKES:** 1½ cups

1 pkg. (8 oz.) reduced-fat cream cheese
½ cup dried cranberries, chopped
½ cup chopped dried apricots
1 tsp. grated orange zest
Assorted crackers

In a large bowl, beat the cream cheese, cranberries, apricots and orange zest until blended. Chill until serving. Serve with crackers.

2 TBSP.: 76 cal., 4g fat (3g sat. fat), 13mg chol., 84mg sod., 9g carb. (6g sugars, 1g fiber), 2g pro.

DIABETIC EXCHANGES: 1 fat, ½ starch.

READER RAVE

"I made this and served it at work. I put it into bite-sized phyllo cups. It went over like gangbusters."
—CHEFETTE13, TASTEOFHOME.COM

ANTIPASTO PLATTER

We entertain often, and antipasto is one of our favorite crowd-pleasers. Guests love having their choice of so many delicious nibbles, including pepperoni and cubes of provolone.
—*Teri Lindquist, Gurnee, IL*

PREP: 10 min. + chilling • **MAKES:** 16 servings (about 4 qt.)

1   jar (24 oz.) pepperoncini, drained
1   can (15 oz.) garbanzo beans or chickpeas, rinsed and drained
2   cups halved fresh mushrooms
2   cups halved cherry tomatoes
½   lb. provolone cheese, cubed
1   can (6 oz.) pitted ripe olives, drained
1   pkg. (3½ oz.) sliced pepperoni
1   bottle (8 oz.) Italian vinaigrette dressing
    Lettuce leaves

1. In a large bowl, combine the pepperoncini, beans, mushrooms, tomatoes, cheese, olives and pepperoni. Pour vinaigrette over mixture; toss to coat.

2. Refrigerate at least 30 minutes or overnight. Arrange on a lettuce-lined platter. Serve with toothpicks.

1 CUP: 178 cal., 13g fat (4g sat. fat), 15mg chol., 852mg sod., 8g carb. (2g sugars, 2g fiber), 6g pro.

SWEET & SAVORY CREAM CHEESE SPREAD

Here's my most popular appetizer. The tempting cheese spread has just the right combo of flavors, but it's the topping that makes it a standout!
—*Lee Ann Miller, Millersburg, OH*

TAKES: 20 min. • **MAKES:** 2 cups

1   pkg. (8 oz.) cream cheese, softened
4   tsp. finely chopped red onion
⅛   tsp. garlic salt
¼   cup butter, cubed
¼   cup packed brown sugar
1   tsp. Worcestershire sauce
½   tsp. yellow mustard
1   cup chopped pecans, toasted
    Assorted crackers

1. In a small bowl, beat cream cheese, onion and garlic salt. Shape into a disk; transfer to a serving plate.

2. In a small saucepan, combine butter, brown sugar, Worcestershire sauce and mustard. Cook and stir over medium heat 4-5 minutes or until the sugar is dissolved. Stir in pecans; cool slightly. Spoon over cheese mixture. Serve with crackers.

2 TBSP.: 140 cal., 13g fat (5g sat. fat), 23mg chol., 83mg sod., 5g carb. (4g sugars, 1g fiber), 2g pro.

APPETIZER WREATH

I always have lots of fun with this festive wreath of topped rolls. Its shape leaves room in the center for another menu item, and I often add a bowl of stuffed olives.
—*Shirley Privratsky, Dickinson, ND*

PREP: 20 min. • **BAKE:** 15 min. + cooling • **MAKES:** 16 servings

2 tubes (8 oz. each) refrigerated crescent rolls
1 pkg. (8 oz.) cream cheese, softened
½ cup sour cream
1 tsp. dill weed
⅛ tsp. garlic powder
1½ cups chopped fresh broccoli florets
½ cup finely chopped sweet red pepper
1 cup finely chopped celery
   Celery leaves

1. Remove the crescent roll dough from the packaging (do not unroll). Cut each tube into 8 slices. Arrange in an 11-in. circle on an ungreased 14-in. pizza pan.

2. Bake at 375° for 15-20 minutes or until golden brown. Cool for 5 minutes before carefully removing to a serving platter; cool completely.

3. In a small bowl, beat cream cheese, sour cream, dill and garlic powder until smooth. Spread on wreath; top with broccoli, red pepper, chopped celery and celery leaves.

1 PIECE: 125 cal., 9g fat (5g sat. fat), 21mg chol., 166mg sod., 7g carb. (2g sugars, 0 fiber), 3g pro.

TEST KITCHEN TIP

Make it Italian! Replace some of the ingredients called for in the recipe with oregano, tomatoes and zucchini. Garnish with basil.

SPICED ORANGE-CRANBERRY CHUTNEY

For me, the aroma of simmering chutney signals the start of the Christmas season.
Try this as an appetizer alongside cream cheese and graham crackers.
—*Pat Stevens, Granbury, TX*

PREP: 15 min. • **COOK:** 55 min. + chilling • **MAKES:** 8 cups

2¼ cups packed brown sugar
1½ cups cranberry juice
½ cup cider vinegar
½ tsp. ground ginger
¼ tsp. ground allspice
3 pkg. (12 oz. each) fresh cranberries
2 Tbsp. grated orange zest
2 medium oranges, peeled and sectioned
1 medium tart apple, peeled and coarsely chopped
½ cup dried currants
½ cup coarsely chopped dried apricots

In a 6-qt. stockpot, combine the first 5 ingredients. Cook, uncovered, over medium heat until the brown sugar is dissolved. Stir in cranberries, orange zest, oranges, apple, currants and apricots. Bring to a boil. Reduce the heat; simmer, uncovered, 50-60 minutes or until thickened, stirring occasionally. Serve chilled.

¼ CUP: 96 cal., 0 fat (0 sat. fat), 0 chol., 7mg sod., 25g carb. (21g sugars, 2g fiber), 0 pro.

ROASTED BEETROOT & GARLIC HUMMUS

This colorful hummus is so tasty, healthy and eye-catching on an appetizer table.
I also make large batches to keep in the fridge for lunches and snacks during the week.
—Elizabeth Worndl, Toronto, ON

PREP: 25 min. • **BAKE:** 45 min. • **MAKES:** 4 cups

- 3 fresh medium beets (about 1 lb.)
- 1 whole garlic bulb
- ½ tsp. salt, divided
- ½ tsp. coarsely ground pepper, divided
- 1 tsp. plus ¼ cup olive oil, divided
- 1 can (15 oz.) garbanzo beans or chickpeas, rinsed and drained
- 3 to 4 Tbsp. lemon juice
- 2 Tbsp. tahini
- ½ tsp. ground cumin
- ½ tsp. cayenne pepper
- ¼ cup plain Greek yogurt, optional
- Minced fresh dill weed or parsley
- Assorted fresh vegetables
- Sliced or torn pita bread

1. Preheat oven to 375°. Pierce beets with a fork; place in a microwave-safe bowl and cover loosely. Microwave beets on high for 4 minutes, stirring halfway. Cool slightly. Wrap beets in individual foil packets.

2. Remove papery outer skin from garlic bulb, but do not peel or separate cloves. Cut in half crosswise. Sprinkle the halves with ¼ tsp. salt and ¼ tsp. pepper; drizzle with 1 tsp. oil. Wrap in individual foil packets. Roast beets and garlic until cloves are soft, about 45 minutes.

3. Remove from oven; unwrap. Rinse beets with cold water; peel when cool enough to handle. Squeeze garlic from skins. Place beets and garlic in a food processor. Add garbanzo beans, lemon juice, tahini, cumin, cayenne pepper and remaining olive oil, salt and ground pepper. Process until smooth.

4. If desired, pulse 2 Tbsp. plain Greek yogurt with beet mixture, dolloping the remaining yogurt over finished hummus. Sprinkle with dill or parsley. Serve with assorted vegetables and pita bread.

¼ CUP: 87 cal., 5g fat (1g sat. fat), 0 chol., 131mg sod., 8g carb. (3g sugars, 2g fiber), 2g pro.

DIABETIC EXCHANGES: 1 fat, ½ starch.

BLUE CHEESE-STUFFED SHRIMP

Jumbo shrimp go from ordinary to extraordinary when you stuff them with a rich mixture of two cheeses, mustard, shallot and parsley. The mild flavor has mass appeal.
—*Amy Dollimount, Glace Bay, NS*

PREP: 20 min. + chilling • **MAKES:** 2 dozen

3 oz. cream cheese, softened
⅔ cup minced fresh parsley, divided
¼ cup crumbled blue cheese
1 tsp. chopped shallot
½ tsp. Creole mustard
24 cooked jumbo shrimp, peeled and deveined

1. In a small bowl, beat the cream cheese until smooth. Beat in ⅓ cup parsley, blue cheese, shallot and mustard. Refrigerate at least 1 hour.

2. Make a deep slit along the back of each shrimp to within ¼-½ in. of the bottom. Stuff with the cream cheese mixture; press remaining parsley onto cream cheese mixture.

1 STUFFED SHRIMP: 43 cal., 2g fat (1g sat. fat), 54mg chol., 89mg sod., 0 carb. (0 sugars, 0 fiber), 6g pro.

DIABETIC EXCHANGES: 1 meat.

5i VODKA-INFUSED CHERRY TOMATOES

These tipsy tomatoes served with seasoned salt for dipping are the perfect way to start a party. The bonus? They take very little time and effort to make!
—*Patricia Nieh, Portola Valley, CA*

PREP: 10 min. + chilling • **MAKES:** 5 dozen

2   pints cherry tomatoes
2   cups vodka
½   cup coarse sea salt, optional
¼   cup coarsely ground pepper, optional

1. Using a skewer, poke a few holes in each tomato. In a container, combine tomatoes and vodka. Cover and refrigerate for 2 days.

2. Pour tomatoes and vodka into a shallow serving dish. Serve tomatoes with toothpicks; if desired, combine sea salt and pepper in a small bowl for dipping.

1 TOMATO: 4 cal., 0 fat (0 sat. fat), 0 chol., 1mg sod., 0 carb. (0 sugars, 0 fiber), 0 pro.

TEST KITCHEN TIP

Add these change-of-pace bites to your Bloody Mary bars at brunches and special get-togethers.

BACON, CHEDDAR & SWISS CHEESE BALL

I get so many requests for this ultimate cheese ball. It is delicious spread on any cracker and makes a fabulous hostess gift, too.
—*Sue Franklin, Lake St. Louis, MO*

PREP: 20 min. + chilling • **MAKES:** 2 cheese balls (4 cups)

1 pkg. (8 oz.) cream cheese, softened
½ cup sour cream
2 cups shredded Swiss cheese
2 cups shredded sharp cheddar cheese
1 cup crumbled cooked bacon (about 12 strips), divided
½ cup chopped pecans, toasted, divided
½ cup finely chopped onion
1 jar (2 oz.) diced pimientos, drained
2 Tbsp. sweet pickle relish
¼ tsp. salt
¼ tsp. pepper
¼ cup minced fresh parsley
1 Tbsp. poppy seeds
   Assorted crackers

1. In a large bowl, beat cream cheese and sour cream until smooth. Stir in shredded cheeses, ½ cup bacon, ¼ cup pecans, onion, pimientos, pickle relish, salt and pepper. Refrigerate, covered, at least 1 hour.

2. In a small bowl, mix the parsley, poppy seeds and remaining bacon and pecans. Spread half the parsley mixture on a large plate. Shape half the cheese mixture into a ball; roll in parsley mixture to coat evenly. Cover. Repeat. Refrigerate at least 1 hour. Serve with crackers.

2 TBSP.: 116 cal., 10g fat (5g sat. fat), 22mg chol., 194mg sod., 2g carb. (1g sugars, 0 fiber), 6g pro.

RECIPE INDEX